T0380286

From
Beckley
to
El Paso
(and **back again**)

A collection of my family's stories

ANNALEE PETERS

WESTBOW
PRESS®
A DIVISION OF THOMAS NELSON
& ZONDERVAN

WestBow Press books may be ordered through booksellers or by contacting:

WestBow Press
A Division of Thomas Nelson & Zondervan
1663 Liberty Drive
Bloomington, IN 47403
www.westbowpress.com
844-714-3454

ISBN: 979-8-3850-2462-9 (sc)
ISBN: 979-8-3850-2463-6 (e)

Library of Congress Control Number: 2024908815

Print information available on the last page.

WestBow Press rev. date: 7/5/2024

A special thank you to everyone who shared stories with me and for those that wish to keep their stories in their hearts. This is for you all. I love you.

FOREWORD

Deuteronomy 32:7 "Remember the days of long ago; think about the generations past. Ask your father and he will inform you. Inquire of your elders and they will tell you." (NLT)

There are some stories in life that captivate us and leave us wanting to know more. My grandmother's story is one of those for me. I had heard about her unusual story of marrying my grandfather when she was only sixteen. I had heard about her traveling by train to meet my then thirty-one-year-old grandfather to be married in El Paso, Texas.

Being a child of the eighties and nineties, I couldn't imagine being ready to travel across the country to marry a man I barely knew. Although this story was unusual to me, I am sure this story was repeated over and over in our country's history during World War II-many marriages were born of necessity during war.

As I have grown older, I have realized that even though this story may have been repeated in history, this story is a part of my very own story. Telling this story through the lens of what my grandmother relayed to me and to others has helped to shape this book into what it is and what it will become to those that read it.

I am sure there are things I will not be able to capture; I wasn't there. There are things that have been shaped in my mind as something that may not be the same to others. However, I hope that this story honors my grandparents' legacies. I know I won't get it all right, not even close. These stories are written in my voice, adapted from what others have told me, written down or shared along the way.

I was able to sit with my grandma a few years before she passed away and record her very own voice telling me some of these special stories. That is one of the greatest gifts she gave me-her stories. I loved talking to her. I was also able to meet with my aunts and dad to retrieve more stories for the book, along with stories handwritten by my uncle that I will also treasure.

My only regret is not having talked more to my grandpa about his life, his story, his side. I was only fourteen when he died and I guess I didn't have the wisdom or maturity to even ask. But maybe some of the things I learned about him were not in stories that he told but in the way he lived, the peculiar way he unwrapped his Christmas and birthday gifts and the way a look could demand everyone stop and pay attention. Even in the way he smiled at us when he didn't think we were watching. Maybe I know more about him than I thought.

I hope this book inspires you to sit and listen to those in your lives, those that have gone before you, soak in the conversations and the stories that they tell you. Don't let these stories end with you. They are a part of you. If you don't tell the story, the story will end.

We forget what we don't take time to remember.

Who's Who

Grandma Scarborough (Harriette Elvira)-Clifford Scarborough's mom (born September 23, 1883-January 1, 1968)

Nita Maxine (Pittman) Scarborough (Grandma, born: August 1, 1927- November 19, 2020)

Clifford Dura Scarborough (Grandpa, born: December 22, 1910-May 23, 1994)

Linda Sue Scarborough (Eldest daughter, 1st born of Clifford and Nita, Born February 5, 1947)

Barbara Ann (Scarborough) Welsh (Middle daughter, 2nd born of Clifford and Nita, Born October 27, 1948)

Jeffrey Neil Scarborough (Eldest son, 3rd born of Clifford and Nita, Born June 23, 1953)

Joan Leigh (Scarborough) Osborne (Youngest daughter, 4th born of Clifford and Nita, Born May 8, 1957)

Clifford David Scarborough (youngest son, 5th born of Clifford and Nita Maxine, Born March 6, 1959)

Grandchildren:

Annalee (Scarborough) Peters (Youngest daughter of Jeffrey Neil Scarborough, Born July 15, 1980)

Angela (Scarborough) Rakes (Oldest daughter of Jeffrey Neil Scarborough, Born January 20, 1977)

Laura (Welsh) Branch (Daughter of Barbara Ann (Scarborough) Welsh, Born January 29, 1977)

Andrew Osborne (Oldest son of Joan (Scarborough) Osborne, Born June 17, 1980)

William Osborne (Youngest son of Joan (Scarborough) Osborne, Born February 13, 1991)

PART ONE

THE TRAIN

Jeremiah 10:23 "I know, Lord, that a man's way of life is not his own; no one who walks determines his own steps. "
(CSB)

"The afternoon knows what the morning never suspected."
- Robert Frost

Boarding the train to El Paso, her heart beat furiously through the white button up blouse she was wearing under her light jacket. A bead of sweat trailed down her back as she gave her ticket to the train conductor. She knew this was what was right and good, but it still felt unbelievably scary. In truth she had no business on this train headed hundreds of miles away. She had never been more than one hundred miles from her small hometown in Beckley, West Virginia. This precious town nestled in the Appalachian Mountains, full of pride and poverty, full of coal and dust.

Yet here she was, her mother had arranged this with Cliff's mother. In reality, she would have done anything to make Cliff's mother happy. Mrs. Scarborough had become like a mother to her. She was kind and caring from the moment she had met her when the family had moved to Ball Street, just a few houses down. Still, this sudden attempt to sure up the foundations of her life and of those around her only made her feel like the foundations of her own world were caving in.

"Ma'am, you need a place to sit?" A good-looking dark-haired man in a uniform looked at her and motioned to the empty seat beside him. She could barely stammer a "Yes, please" before she sat, and he began talking to her. The man was traveling home before his next deployment to see his family. He went on and on about his wife and the new baby she had just given birth to, showing a wrinkled picture of a red-faced little boy in an auburn haired woman's lap. He talked quickly and intently about his life, he seemed nervous, probably most soldiers felt this way at one time or another. The honest thought of realizing this could be the last time to hold your wife's hand or smell the scent of your newborn child must have weighed heavily on the soul.

The train began to fill more and more quickly as soldiers from several branches boarded. She couldn't help but notice some of the men in uniforms, their broad backs and muscular arms. It made her blush. She tried not to stare at the people boarding but it was all so new to her. She had taken the bus from Beckley, West Virginia to Prince, West Virginia to catch the train. This was almost further already than she had ever traveled in her life.

She had always been timid, the quiet one. Her sister had been the one to lead the conversations, introducing herself and her little sister last. She had always lived in that shadow, and what a shadow it had been. She loved her sister; she knew this to be true but there were definite rough patches in their relationship that needed mending. That aside, she had excelled in her studies in school, always getting good grades, often being the brunt of jokes and being called the "teacher's pet". To her that was ok. She knew where she stood and there was a sense of security in that, knowing what others expected and achieving those expectations. She never veered far off course and always made good decisions. She was level-headed and at sixteen, ready to take on the role of a wife.

But was she really? Her thoughts roamed anxiously through her mind as she felt the train lurch ahead and the last calls were made to board. The man who had been chattering beside her finally looked at her and asked, "What takes you on the train, ma'am?" The question was simple, yet she could say so many things. "I am actually going to El Paso, Texas." She offered with little explanation. "El Paso?! Well, what's a little thing like you heading there alone? You do know there's a war going on right?" She laughed at his slight joke. You would have had to be hidden under a rock to not know there was a war going on. "Of course, sir," she blushed and held back a slight smile as her eyes brimmed with tears. She wasn't sure where the sudden emotion came from. "I am going to meet my fiancé to be married. He's stationed in El Paso with the army." After some brief conversation, the man turned away with a distant look in his eyes. It was like that during those times. You could be talking to someone one minute and the next, they were thinking about someone or something that they had lost or had to leave because of this war. It was one of the hardest times for everyone in the country, in the world. It went without saying.

She looked ahead and noticed a paper peeking out from the seat in front of her. The patron had left it hanging over the edge of their seat. The headline on the paper read, "The Invasion of Normandy". The huge black letters seemed to glare back at her face. The news was unsettling as she had no idea what this would mean for her very own life. What if the man she would marry would be called out to some other part of the world, leaving her all alone to fend for herself? It was something she couldn't worry about yet. She just needed to get to him first. This June 6th, 1944 was not only D Day for the US Allied forces on the beaches of Normandy, this was a D Day in the life of a 16 year old girl, traveling across the country to initiate the start of a new life.

She listened to the chatter and commotion around her on the train. Mostly the men talking, some women and children, flitting about. The sounds of train engines, the conductor and the bells chiming arrival times and departures. She suddenly missed the sounds of the old street, the street that she had come to love, the street she grew up on.

She closed her eyes and rested her head on the back of her seat, all the while envisioning running up and down with her sister to the neighbors' houses. She had vivid memories of the races that the boys down the street would have while trying to impress the girls. The small stoop she would sit on as she talked to Mrs. Scarborough came to mind. She loved that woman. She was so kind and listened with a heart of grace. When she felt invisible to the world around her, this woman, more than thirty years her senior, would invite her to sit and talk, to drink iced tea, to help fold clothes off the line.

Whatever they did, they would talk, and Mrs. Scarborough would listen. She would really listen, without interrupting, without assumptions. She had become a second mother to her. She would give anything to transport herself to that old porch stoop on Ball Street, to sit with Mrs. Scarborough or help her with her laundry. But here she was, traveling across the country to marry this precious woman's son.

A Proposal of Sorts

The arrangement had been made. It was one of necessity and love. War made these things a necessity, love made you follow through. She followed through because she knew it was the right thing to do in the eyes of her family, she carried through because she loved her own mother, and she loved Mrs. Scarborough. She thought that maybe the love you feel for someone else can simply carry you to love the people that you're supposed to love.

She remembered the first time she had met him. He was handsome with bright blue eyes. He was only home briefly from a job across town, and he was due to head out to basic training later that month. He always seemed to be busy and working, focused on something other than what was right there in front of him.

She was young and even though she realized he was attractive; it wasn't in the way a sixteen-year-old realizes. It was the way a ten-year-old looks at the mailman, or in this case, Mrs. Scarborough's son. He was plenty attractive, but he was grown up and had no time to engage in conversations with neighborhood kids. Cliff was mysterious to all the kids her age. He came and went as older children in a family do. Coming to see their parents on a holiday but it wasn't often that he was there or maybe that no one noticed. He was quiet, never calling attention to himself so you probably wouldn't notice his comings and goings. He was serious. Too serious for a ten-year-old to really notice.

Fast forward life and time, and now she was serious too. The whole country had become serious. Serious about our country, protecting it, protecting our families. Serious about rations, serious about everything. So here she was in this serious business of becoming a wife. Cliff had been in town previously and presented a ring. It was a memory she wouldn't likely forget.

It was a Friday, and she was walking home from school with her sister and some other neighborhood friends. She had had a long week, lots of tests and an earache that wouldn't seem to go away. She was tired of hearing about the war, the drills at school to make all the students hide under their desks. She was tired of making plans to head to Ohio to finish her high school years as she helped in a BF Goodrich factory. She just wanted to finish her schooling like "normal people" she had told her mother. Her mother reminded her that not much was normal these days.

She had been aimlessly kicking a rock when she saw him. He was standing beside the front door to her house. He had been sitting with his mother. Mrs. Scarborough beamed at her as she waved. She approached the steps, Mrs. Scarborough and Cliff. He smiled and his bright blue eyes lit up when he saw her. "I have to talk to you." He stole a quick glance at his mother, and she waved again mentioning housework and walked back across the street. "Can we take a walk?" He was clearly agitated or nervous. She couldn't tell which. "Sure, let me just set these books down and let my dad know." She ran inside, not knowing the conversation she was about to have would change her life. Her own life, Cliff's life and their family's lives, forever.

The screen door slammed as she ran back out the door. Her face colored as she took in the handsome man waiting for her. She had known him all her life. They had grown up on the same street, but their lives were different. For one, he was older and, in the military, now, only coming home to see his parents on leave and between assignments. He was also quiet and different than others she knew. He was like a page from an old book, like when someone had torn it out because it was special but not really knowing exactly why.

She smiled and they began their walk down the road. His pace quickened and she struggled to follow. "You know the war is going on and things are really hard right now for a lot of people." He started in on his speech that seemed almost practiced, rehearsed. She looked at him in a sideways glance and chuckled, "Yes, you would have to be completely detached from the world to not know the war was happening and yes, things are hard, for everyone, even me. I must head to Ohio to finish up high school and help out in the BF Goodrich plant. Mom says it's temporary and will be helpful to make money for the family. Like "killing two birds with one stone" she says." He smiled a sad smile and looked at the dirt below them. "Everyone is making sacrifices, Nita. That's what I want to talk to you about.

Not really sacrifices but something that may be helpful in the end but may change things a lot right now."

At this point, she could feel the stiffer way he was walking and sense the tension in his voice. She was scared to ask what he was thinking so she didn't. She just waited. "I want you to marry me. Your parents want to make sure you are taken care of, and my mom loves you like her own already. It makes sense. A lot of people are doing this now. It would be for the good of each other and our families." He stopped and placed his right hand just above her left forearm. The gesture seemed out of place, it was kind and good but not really telling of anything. This whole conversation was out of place, and she wanted to place her hands over her ears and cry, to shut it all out, to run away kicking and screaming. But she was a grown woman now, it seemed, ready for a proposal of sorts that she never saw coming.

She looked his way and almost as if she saw through him, she tried to imagine the people in their lives surrounding them as they got older, their families laughing around them at holidays and birthdays, maybe even a child or two playing at her feet as she cooked and tidied the house, a house she didn't yet know, but could only imagine. Isn't this what every girl wants? Yet she felt like it was all wrong, arranged by those around her while she was trying to live a "normal" teenage life during this war. She was stunned and taken aback, so far back really that it would take years to bring her back to her place in this life. So, she said the only thing she knew to say and the only thing expected of her, "Yes." With that, she turned around and began the walk back home. Tears streamed down her face as she ignored the sound of his voice calling for her to stop, with a ring in his hand.

Missing Luggage

She had only rested her eyes for a minute, or at least that's what it had felt like. She felt the train come to a stop with a jolt that sent her head forward and the bag she had been clutching in her lap to the floor. She heard a voice of the train conductor as he piped out the stop on the loudspeaker. She smelled the heavy scents of aftershave, cigarette smoke, perfume and baby powder.

She focused her eyes on the gentleman who had helped her with her luggage when there was a brief stop. She laughed to herself recalling the sight she must have been to the man and the conductor. She had needed to find a restroom during a brief stop and unbeknownst to her, there was a car switch. This meant that you had to pull your luggage to a new car during the brief layover. She had asked the gentleman beside her to keep an eye on her bag as she went to a restroom. As always, her anxiety got the best of her when she returned and saw no one in the car and her luggage was gone too.

Her heart beat out of her chest, and she found the closest worker to her old train car and simply asked, "Have you seen a man with luggage in a uniform?" The worker laughed and pointed all around them at the various men in uniform, carrying all sorts of luggage pieces. Her face burned bright red as she realized what she had done. She and the man laughed, and she thanked him as she felt the hand of someone on her shoulder. "I have your luggage right here miss." She turned around to meet the kind hazel eyes of the soldier she had met earlier on the journey and entrusted her luggage. She laughed and breathed a sigh of relief as she took the suitcase handle, thanked him and wished him well on his journey. She would never see him again in her life, but she often wondered about him and his family, hoping he had been able to get home to see his wife and meet his new baby.

Her mind came reeling back to reality as the conductor continued to call out their whereabouts and stops. She was in El Paso, Texas. She felt like the ride had been forever in some ways and just minutes in others. She was amazed and almost proud of the fact that she had made it this far, on her own.

She stretched as she moved out of her seat. She pulled her luggage and bag to her as she remembered the plan that had been given to her before she even set foot on this journey. Cliff would be waiting at the train depot. She would step off the train and possibly have to wait for a while or maybe he would be right there, with flowers in hand, smiling. She had no clue which it would be. The flowers part she had dreamed up, maybe he would be romantic though.

She was immediately hit with the oppressive heat of Texas and the bright sun made her squint her eyes as she stepped down off the car. She almost missed the last step off the train when she felt a hand by her side, hoisting her down. She looked up and saw him, right there. She wouldn't have to wait at all.

El Paso

The next few days would be a blur for her, for both of them. She was a married woman now. She wondered if anyone could look at her and just know, know that she was no longer just Nita Maxine Pittman but Mrs. Nita Maxine

Scarborough. Probably not. She felt her face creep with color as her thoughts wondered to her husband and his kindness the first few days together. Her mind wondered back to the actual day they made their nuptial agreements. It was probably the most "normal" thing she would do in years.

After she had literally stumbled off the train car, exhausted from travel and too hot to think straight, Cliff had taken her to lunch in a nearby restaurant. They had used the time to catch up on life as they told each other about what was happening in both West Virginia and Texas. She filled him in on his mother and he told her about the gun drills and new people he seemed to constantly be meeting on base. He complained about the food as he bit into a hamburger dripping with ketchup, grinning as he wiped the grease from his mouth. She was in shock, sitting in front of this blue-eyed man that would soon be her husband. She was so used to being his friend or neighbor, she was scared the new title "wife" would be hard to live up to.

They knew their time was limited together. Cliff had not even gotten permission to go off base for his soon to be bride. His good buddy, Joe, was making sure he called out his name if roll was taken that day. It was a risk, but he took it, at least for this day.

They made their way to the El Paso Courthouse in El Paso County, Texas. The huge white building with its wide columns was just the backdrop one would think of for getting married. At least that's what she thought as she climbed the steps, surrounded with men and women coming and going from the same building. She had to catch her breath as they walked into the courthouse building, not because of the steps but because of what she knew was about to happen, what was about to change her life forever. She was going to leave this building with a new last name.

They entered the main area, labeled with specific names and areas located within the courthouse. Knowing that they would need to see a Justice of the Peace, they tried to locate that. Having no luck and most likely looking very confused, a kind woman came up to them. "Hello, you all look like you can use some help." She smiled brightly under a haze of brown curly hair and light round glasses that framed her eyes and barely fit onto the tip of her nose.

"Yes, we need to find a Justice of the Peace to be married." Cliff spoke in a matter of fact manner as he would do the rest of his life, Nita would witness many times after that day.

"Indeed, well, I'm afraid that there is no one here to help with that today…." Her voice trailed off as she glanced across the hall to a larger room. Cliff and Nita followed her gaze to a larger room than the one they were in, yet one that looked like a small, stately courtroom. A large, balding man sat at a desk.

Just as they were about to turn their heads, the balding man turned to catch their hawking eyes and a large smile passed over his entire face, even lighting his eyes. "Nancy, you sure know how to keep a man busy on his hour off." He winked at the little woman with the brown hair and small glasses as her face reddened at the sound of his voice.

"Mr. Scarborough, these two need to be married." She winked at him. Nita wondered why she was calling him Mr. Scarborough because that was Cliff's last name, not this man's last name! She also wondered if this was their usual office banter and felt as if she was intruding on a private conversation.

"Well enough, Nancy. Who do we have here?" His eyes sizing up both Cliff and Nita, making note of the very thing he saw most days, two young people, set on getting married before one went off to war and the other home to wait, to wait and wonder and hope. He gestured for them to follow him through the doors to his office.

"My name is Mr. Alvin Scarborough, El Paso County court judge, and I have a few minutes so I wouldn't mind helping you two out. Can I get a little more information from the both of you?" He smiled and pulled out papers that he probably handled more lately than not. He put both of them at ease with his Texas drawl and kind eyes. As they explained that they wanted to be married, Cliff was stationed on base in El Paso and that their name was Scarborough too, they all seemed to relax and chuckled at the irony of having the same last name.

The judge asked them a few more questions, they signed some papers stating who they were and the intent of the visit today. As the rights of marriage were read to them, they looked at each other, knowing that their lives would never be the same. They just had no idea how different it would be.

Wedding Day Dinner

They left the courthouse knowing their time together was short because Cliff had left base, basically AWOL. His buddies had told them they would answer roll calls for him if they needed to. The sun was blazing hot as they walked down the streets of El Paso. They had wanted to look for a place to eat before they had to get to the hotel for the night. Cliff's buddies had recommended a place in the heart of El

Paso-a restaurant specializing in Chinese cuisine. Chinese food was not common in southern West Virginia at the time so neither Cliff nor Nita had really eaten it before. Despite their lack of knowledge of good Chinese cuisine, they decided to take the recommendation of Cliff's friends. They arrived at the restaurant and noticed that you had to go in the back entrance, there was not an actual front entryway. As they made their way from the kitchen in the back of the restaurant to the front to be seated, their senses were assaulted. The smell of rotten meat sitting in the heat in the outdoor trash cans wafted to their noses, the flies buzzing near the raw meat and vegetables along with the sounds of Chinese being spoken and yelled back and forth in the kitchen was like a mad symphony to their ears.

They sat quietly and were handed water in glasses that looked as though they had a greasy coating on the outsides. They couldn't really tell if they were drinking water or not. They looked around, being the only white, non-Asians in the restaurant, feeling sorely out of place. They lingered over their water before they said at the same time, "Do you think it's okay if we find another place to eat?" They both fell back in their seats laughing, getting a few looks from other patrons but they really didn't care. They eventually found a small steak house where they had their first married meal. They often wondered if Cliff's friends had set them up for a good laugh. They would never know because Cliff decided never to tell his friends that they had gone there.

When he did return from his "honeymoon" his friends did tell him that he had been paged while he was gone. He had had a physical the day before in which he had to give a urine sample. Apparently, the sample went missing and they needed more urine the day he was gone. One of his friends produced a urine sample for him so he wouldn't get in trouble. Cliff often laughed at that. Despite how mischievous his friends had been, they always took care of him.

The Early Years

The years went by. They flew by. With five children, life gets busy. It was always that way really- in the beginning when they returned from Texas and even before that, before they were living life in the small, cramped house at 210 Hedrick Street.

Nita could remember the first time they set foot in the small house. The house that would see them through births, deaths, sicknesses, job changes, wars, and everyday normal things like getting up for school with children fighting over bathrooms. She laughed thinking about how naive they were in the beginning.

The previous owners, The Borden's, had been divorced and had moved to Florida. Almost everything that they couldn't pack quickly had been left in the house- including dishes and linens. What most would consider an inconvenience in today's age, was a blessing to them then.

Most people would want to go into a new home these days, fill it with things that suited their tastes and decor ideas. However, during the 1940's and the height of World War II, having these necessities meant less work on their part, scouring the department stores to see if they could even find the items they needed. In so many cases, back then, you could only get one or two place settings and most tables were a mismatched set of dishes, just thankful to have what they had- family around the table and food to fill their bellies.

When Nita thought back to her first impression of the house, she chuckled. She remembered walking into the small home and immediately the smell of something sour and possibly rotten filling her nose. She told Cliff, "You may have to go first. I want to be sure that if someone has died here, I'm not the one to see their body first." Cliff took a stance at the door in front of her and scanned the living area downstairs. "All clear down here so far." He had looked behind at her as if to say, "You'll be safe. Don't worry."

He entered the house and as he made his way to the kitchen, he yelled out, "I found it!" She ran in behind him having to cover her nose with her hand as she clamped her mouth shut so as not to gag. She looked over into the kitchen sink and saw the culprit of the smell. The water had been sitting stagnant in the sink after some type of plumbing issue had backed it up for days. It was black and murky and looked like something straight out of a swamp.

She ran to the back door to open it and let fresh air circulate in the kitchen. She gulped in the fresh air as Cliff rolled up his sleeves to investigate the sink, like this was all in a day's work for him, like he didn't even smell the putrid smell wafting through the house. She remembered him like that though. Solid, factual, and always ready to work and fix what needed to be fixed in a situation.

She left him to it as she roamed the house. She walked around to find the bedrooms and a bathroom. She looked out the windows, taking it all in, daydreaming about how the neighbors would wave hello to them as they passed by, thinking about the dinners that would be cooked in the small kitchen, with family around the table.

She was snapped out of her daydreams as Cliff yelled for her to come help him. "Nita, come here and hold this flashlight. I need to see straight to the bottom to make sure I can unclog this sink." She sighed and left the window daydreaming where it was, she was a wife now and her husband needed her.

PART TWO

SHORT STORIES ABOUT LIFE

Nita Maxine-Remodeling

---

*"The house don't fall when the bones
are good."-Maren Morris*

The house was just too small. We needed the room for all seven of us, for us to live and be and breathe. Some days it was suffocating. The laundry was always piled up, my fingers were always calloused from taking the laundry from the ringer washer to the outside line, hanging each garment one at a time. Eventually these same clothes would be taken back inside, often frozen in the winter. I would fold and place them in the gas oven to season them and make sure they were dry. Barbara and Linda would help but it wasn't their jobs to do, they were only kids themselves. This work fell to a mother, to me. Often days I would look around and wonder how we had come this far in these little rooms, in this little house.

I remember talking to Cliff about remodeling the house. He knew it was a necessity but he also knew it would cost money. I knew he would end up doing it all by himself, with the help of some neighbors, family, and friends, but mostly Cliff. He was a proud man, and he would get the work done.

The first hole went into the wall and my heart shattered. Would it always be a mess here? Would we ever have memories of anything new? There were days I thought that I would go mad with the holes in the walls and construction, but I knew it was a necessary evil to have a larger space for everyone.

There was a day when the whole house was braced on jacks and lifted to complete the basement area that would years later hold the washer and dryer, a desk area for Cliff's paperwork and even more storage space. I had no idea a house could be lifted on jacks like a car but I learned something new that day.

As Cliff, Elbert Lee, and some other Pack family members gathered around the house at the points at which they would literally turn the handle on the jack to lift the house, my heart beat out of my chest. What if the whole blasted house fell apart? Now, that would be one for the books. But it didn't happen that way. The men shouted, "Turn!" and at that command, every man turned as to not get the house out of alignment. I took in the grimaces on their faces, the sweat and dirt and frustration, until it was finally just right and finished, every man breathing hard with sweat dripping down their red faces.

I can't remember the exact day that "the new part" of the house was completely finished but I remember the kitchen, with the oven and range being on one side of the kitchen, opening up to the sink under the window that looked out the back yard. The space for a dining table and extra living room. It was perfect. It was worth it.

Nita Maxine-A boy and his dog

"Dog's lives are too short. Their only fault, really." -Agnes Sligh Turnbull

---

She had never seen a boy love a dog more than Jeff loved Gypsy. It was an unusual occurrence to see them apart. Gypsy would lag behind Jeff most days that he wandered around the neighborhood. She was both his watch dog and constant companion. Gypsy was a shaggy haired little mutt of a dog, she was high strung, just about as high strung as the boy she chased daily. Jeff was the third born child to Nita and Cliff Scarborough. He was the third of five children. The one smack dab in the middle who needed no introduction because he never met a stranger. As soon as he woke up in the mornings until he fell completely dead asleep at night, the boy was moving.

Jeff grew up, like all little boys do and so did Gypsy. Gypsy became old, tired, slower, and could hardly see. It was David, Jeff's brother, who finally made the decision to put Gypsy down. Jeff couldn't bear to do it.

She remembered looking at Gypsy, remembering her as if she had been a puppy, nipping at everyone's heels, teaching the kids responsibility, watching Gypsy grow old and tired as her family grew up too. Jeff was hardly around anymore and he knew Gypsy's health was declining. He knew it was time to say goodbye even though saying goodbye to one of the first things you ever loved is hard, even if you aren't that little rambunctious boy anymore.

She looked out the window, one of the windows that she often liked to gaze out as she prayed or daydreamed and saw David. She heard the beating of the earth as he dug a hole large enough and deep enough for Gypsy's small body. She noticed the somber way his shoulders sagged as he wiped sweat from his forehead. She wanted to run out and offer him water or tea, or some type of comfort. Instead, she stood there, finally wiping a lone tear that ran down her cheek, turned from the window and started dinner.

NITA MAXINE-HIGH SCHOOL

*"The roots of education are bitter, but
the fruit is sweet." Aristotle*

High School is a rite of passage for some, high school in her case was a box to check, a period in her life to get through while she waited for the rest of her life to begin.

Nita Maxine Pittman attended high school in Akron, Ohio. Her family had decided that it was wise to move here during the war to be near other families and to take advantage of the work that was provided in some of the largest rubber producing factories in the world like B.F. Goodrich.

She was a good student, did her lessons and turned in her work. She did what was expected and tried not to complain, although sometimes at night, she would have complete conversations with her pillow about how hard being in high school, trying to graduate with honors and working in a factory truly was. She would complain about how unfair it was, and then she would realize she had a mother and a father and family who loved her and only wanted the best for her. She thought about so many families ripped apart by the war and she would immediately feel selfish for her rants, albeit only to a pillow.

She remembered how she felt like such an outsider, a complete bumpkin, as she walked down the hall at school from English class to her math class earlier that day. She had hidden her face from the stares and the comments she heard from others asking, "Who's the new girl?" It was only when she dropped her math book and scrambled to pick it up, that she made eye contact with a girl that looked to be in her class, near the same age-sixteen or seventeen.

"Uh…hi, sorry. Excuse me," she said quickly, hoping not to make a scene and just get to class. The girl looked up at her through dark brown eyes, reminding her of the color of coffee, her long blond hair that had been curled and pinned back. She was dressed smartly and looked happy enough to be heading down the hall to her next class. She winked at Nita and asked, "What's your next course? I may be headed that way. I can show you the way."

"Math-um, Mr. Smith's Algebra course." Nita muttered quietly and looked down. "I know exactly where Mr. Smith's class is and I'm actually in that class as well." She quickly linked arms with Nita, and they headed down the hall. Suddenly, the gazes of others seemed to fade. If they were talking about the new girl, she didn't hear it anymore. Nita had just made her first friend in Akron.

Nita Maxine-War Work

> *"There is one front and one battle where everyone*
> *in the United States-every man, woman, and child-*
> *is in action, and will be privileged to remain in*
> *action throughout this war. That front is right here*
> *at home, in our daily lives, and in our daily tasks."*
> President Franklin D. Roosevelt (April 28, 1942)

Working in the B.F. Goodrich plant during the war seemed like the "right" thing to do. It was like I was doing, we were all doing, our part to help in the war effort without being on the front lines. I couldn't be with Cliff and communication often took weeks. I never knew if he was truly alright or if he had been gunned down flying over some enemy territory. Quite frankly, I never really knew exactly where he was. I think it was supposed to be that way. However, this small effort to help the war made me feel closer to him, like I was doing something right, good, even noble.

The first day was the hardest. I was sixteen and full of my own opinions and knowledge, but I knew nothing about this business of creating and shipping rubber goods for the war.

After arriving at the plant, I was taken to a room called the "Debriefing Room". I had been placed in the chemistry department of the plant because I had good grades in chemistry. I was not sure how high school chemistry would help me with the production of rubber at the BF Goodrich Plant but apparently someone thought that it would.

I listened to a middle-aged man drone on about rubber and polymers and the production of rubber as our responsibility for helping in the war effort. I was close to drifting off to sleep when another young girl caught my eye and waved in my direction. I quickly snapped out of the fog that had enveloped me and slightly smiled at the girl.

After our debrief and explanation of our job duties, I met the young girl out in the hallway as we made our way to a small picnic area outside of the rear of the plant where we would eat lunch. She extended her hand as we walked along, "Hey there, my name's Hope, Hope Everheart. Was it just me or did that debrief need to be a bit briefer?" She winked and gave me a sideways smile and laugh. I glanced back at the group, making sure no one could see me agree with her, though I thought it was horribly long as well. I just didn't want to get in trouble. I shook her hand briefly and answered, "Yes, it was a long bit of information."

We walked to a table and sat together as Hope continued to talk, "I hope you don't mind me sitting with you. I figure us girls better stick together." It was like we had been friends for a long time. We ate and talked. Hope asked me about where I had come from, she told me she had lived in Akron all her life and even had a car. By the end of the conversation, we had already planned a trip to a local park the following Saturday. She had wanted to show me the area and let me meet some of her friends.

We finished lunch and walked back into the plant to finish our shift. The rest of the day consisted of more meetings and explanations as to what we would be doing when we came to work. It was a long day, but it certainly went by much more quickly knowing I had Hope by my side.

LINDA-HOPE

"Friendship isn't about being inseparable, but about being separated and knowing nothing will change." Unknown

---

I remembered the cards; I think all the kids did. I was the oldest, so I had seen most of them. I remember how mom got so excited when one would come in the mail. She would almost shimmy slide back from the mailbox like a dance. It was like a grand surprise for her, like a story she had been waiting to read, that only came once a year. Those cards were a reminder to me that my mom had had a life before all of us, before our little home on Hedrick Street filled with lots of kids and never quite enough room for everything. It's a strange notion when you realize you are not the sum of who your parents are, that they were people before they were parents.

This yearly letter was a joy to us all as we watched a smile dance over mom's face, and she would read them aloud to all of us. We would sit around, listening wide-eyed, like we were listening to the life happenings of a movie star.

Her good friend, Hope Everheart of Akron, Ohio, would write yearly around Christmas time and include her letter with a pretty card. She would tell of her life and things happening in Ohio, her immediate family and their comings and goings. Mom and Hope had worked together in the B.F. Goodrich Plant in Akron years ago, during the war, after she had married dad and then moved there to finish up her senior year of high school.

These letters made mom smile and even laugh at times. There were things Hope would say that I didn't quite find so funny, and I'm sure none of the others did either, but mom would giggle like a schoolgirl. I'm pretty sure some of the words Hope wrote were like private jokes, maybe funny things they would talk about when they were working shoulder to shoulder years ago. I wonder how they truly met. Mom just said, "We worked together". I had wanted more details but sometimes you are not privy to those things. I think the time that bound mom and Hope together was the most difficult time of their lives. Maybe mom didn't really want to remember the work, but the silver lining of a friend that she had met in that dark space of time.

It was in the early 2000's and Hope was turning eighty years old. She was having a birthday party and the Christmas cards that mom would get yearly, even after all these years, had turned into a card of invitation. Hope would turn eighty that summer and mom wanted to go. Mom was still driving around town, although I wasn't always sure she should, but driving to Akron, Ohio alone was something else. After some wavering back and forth, it was settled. I would take mom. I was excited to do this. I had just moved back to West Virginia from Colorado and I was happy to be needed by my family. I had missed them and was excited to meet the Hope that had imprinted upon my mom's life and heart for all these years.

I drove and mom held onto the door handle tightly. She complained that my Colorado driving was much more aggressive than her own. We went back and forth and I realized that some arguments are not worth winning. We stopped at a few places to rest and eat lunch and about six hours later, we pulled into the hotel we would stay in that night after Hope's party. The hotel was interesting to say the least, it was a grand place adjoined to a circular building, much like an old silo. Me and mom got a kick out of saying we were staying in a silo for the night.

It was a beautiful event at a downtown restaurant. There was a back room devoted to large parties and this one had been decorated tastefully with flowers and balloons to celebrate the life of an eighty-year-old. There were pictures scattered around of a girl, then a grown woman and also an elderly woman-all Hope, wide eyes and smiling the same mischievous smile in all of them. I stood back during the event, making small talk with some of Hope's family members, eating the meal, clapping for this woman as speeches were made and toasts were clinked.

I could tell Hope was the type of person if you met once, it was like knowing her forever-you would always, in some way, be hers. She made people feel special, I could tell that, even as I had only just met her, she took my hand and gently embraced me, telling me she was thankful I had brought my mother. She was kind like that and even at the age of eighty, it felt like she was taking care of everyone at the party-flitting from table to table and group to group for small talk, hugs and making sure everyone had enough to eat and drink.

I noticed that Hope had never had children but, in more ways than one, her friends and their families were like her very own, with children all over the place. She had loved to travel and many of the photos were of her in various places that I am sure mom loved to hear about in her letters. I did notice that night that as Hope walked around, almost floating really, with a smile on her face, she had a terrible cough. At one point it was all she could do to contain it as she walked outside for some fresh air.

The best of it all was mom. Just watching mom in her element with Hope was like a balm to my heart. I had often wondered about mom. I had known her in the beginning. The beginning of motherhood, in the thick of it all, figuring out how to be a mother and wife and just be. Trying to stitch things together when they all but fell apart. That was mom, always working and going and doing, to an exhaustive bend. I had hoped she had, at one point, had this special connection with someone. Now, I see she did.

As I took a picture of them beaming together under a banner that said "Happy 80th Birthday!" with my new digital camera, I choked back a tear that tried to escape. It's a beautiful thing to see a glimpse of a person that you never even knew existed. Hope had given my mom joy at a time in her life when she really needed it. I understood those letters now, their meaning, the true meaning of their lifelong friendship and I will be forever grateful for that.

Barbara-Washing Machine Woes

We called the lot "El Paso". It was just an old dirt lot that was a magical place of daydreams for us. El Paso was the city in Texas we had heard many stories about as we grew up. El Paso was the city where my mom and dad were married, the place my mom traveled to when she was only sixteen; the place that would change her life forever and the place that we daydreamed about. We knew El Paso was like the "wild west" we had seen a few times on television in the old westerns or at least that's what we envisioned it to be like. Maybe that was part of the romantic idea of it all- this place we had only heard about and had never seen, yet it was a part of what made us who we were.

As my bike trailed down the last bit of road into the old dirt lot, I was greeted by a few neighborhood friends. Snow had begun to fall, and we knew that this could be the last time we played without a new blanket of fresh, white snow beneath us. We played tag and opened our mouths to catch snowflakes. This lot was our home away from home, our special place. I prayed we would be able to keep it ours for years, even though I was already starting to feel too grown up to play there, it always drew me back in. What seemed like only minutes, turned into hours and the sun began to set and I made my way back home, wondering if we would be able to sled down Kessinger's hill tomorrow.

I was greeted by mom as I entered the front door and the smell of cooking dinner. I knew it was time for me to help and I thought ahead to the chores and homework that awaited me. So often I felt overwhelmed but not at this moment. Christmas break was only a few days away and there was a tangible feeling of excitement here and everywhere I went. Mom always loved Christmas and made it special, no matter what we did or did not have. I felt a warmth in my bones tonight.

Our house was always loud and full. Tonight was no different. I helped mom get dinner on the table and as we sat and ate, I almost felt like I was looking down on the whole scene. This house, so small, yet so full of life, mom always moving about and dad always working and tinkering on some project. We were like a small source of light on this little street. I wondered if anyone else ever felt that way. I smiled and mom asked me to help get the clothes in the wash to which I dutifully responded, "Sure mom."

Mom always kept the play clothes separate from our "good" clothes-especially the ones she worked hard to sew and create for us. There were always patterns for dresses and pants scattered around the sewing machine from the Piece Goods store in Beckley. As I loaded the washer with the clothes and soap, I absentmindedly put my hand near the ringers above the barrel as I smiled and hummed a Christmas carol that had been on the fringes of my mind all day. Before I realized what was happening, an intense pain shot through my hand and up my arm. I was stuck in the ringers of the washer. I had no idea what happened next, but I was screaming at the top of my lungs. Where in the world had dad and everyone else gone? Outside to check on something in the garage? To the store? I couldn't remember. I had been so focused on my chores and what I had to do, on Christmas break, on the sweet feeling of it all.

The kitchen door flung open, and mom stood there with her mouth wide open and her eyes startled. "Barbara Ann! What are you doing?!" She ran to my side, quickly realizing my hand was stuck in the wringers and released them. I pulled my hand out and stretched it in front of my face to see if there was any damage. Fingers and hands still intact, I looked at mom and smiled as I wiped the tears of pain and laughter from my cheeks. "Thanks mom. That could have been bad." She hugged me and laughed, "Yes, it could have. Thank goodness I was here. You must be much more careful next time." She reprimanded me but she also held me a little longer and hugged me a little tighter than she usually did.

Joan-My Baby

*"In some ways, siblings, especially sisters,
are more influential in your childhood than
your parents." Deborah Tannen*

David was the best gift my parents could bring home. I remember when he came home, my earliest memories of mom included "my baby". I staked my claim on this baby angel from day one. I felt a sense of responsibility for this new little boy that I will never be able to explain. The smell of a baby and the duties of a mother intrigued me at such a young age.

At the point that David and I came around, Barbara and Linda were older. They had bossed Jeff and me around for long enough; it was my turn. I remember the feeling of helping David-helping him as he learned to walk, playing with him, even helping mom feed and diaper him. The two of us watching Captain Kangaroo while munching on cinnamon toast. To this day, cinnamon toast can still transport me back in front of the television set with my little brother. That is what he was to me- "my little brother" in every sense of the statement. He was mine and I loved him so.

I wonder what it would be like starting over again like that as parents. Half of your kids are grown and the other half in elementary school, preschool and diapers. I just know there was never a day I didn't see my mom working hard to provide for us. She worked tirelessly, like the nights I would see her sewing our holiday outfits with matching coats as we all went to bed. She somehow still had energy to exercise-even before it was a popular thing to do. She would jump around or stretch in front of the television taking her cues from the famous Jack LaLane.

Somehow, she was up and ready before us all. Mom's energy was tireless and I hoped one day I would have a baby just like David and be like her. Maybe not just like her but I knew she was a good mom, she cared, she was there, she helped to provide. I knew things were different for her by the time I came along, and then David. She was back at school, learning a new role in a life that had always told her what role she had to play.

JEFF AND DAVID-HUNTING

---

*"Good things come to those who wait."-an old
ketchup commercial and hunters in the woods*

Hunting is something we have always done. It's not the
kind of thing we think too much about, unless we can't do
it and then we wish we were in the middle of the woods
somewhere, hunting. We had an old hunting dog named
Lady and we decided to take her rabbit hunting.

We loaded up the truck and headed to the water reservoir
in Ghent where we hunted often. We took Lady to see if she
would scrounge up any rabbits for the day. Lady was pretty
persistent and once she had a rabbit in her sights, she would
spend all day and every last ounce of her energy chasing it.

One we got to our hunting spot, we let Lady go and do
her thing. She found a few rabbits that day, but we never
could get a clear shot on one. Lady had a ball though,
yipping and calling out when she would find a rabbit.

We decided to call it a day and as we trudged back to the
truck, no prizes in hand for the day, we passed an old shed. It
was really an old lean-to that was falling down. As we passed
by the shed, a turkey flew out of the side and hit the ground
running. Dad threw up his shot gun and the next thing we

know, he is shooting at the turkey. We are all so excited at this point, that all three of us start shooting at the turkey.

We were so excited after a day with nothing to show for our efforts that we completely lost all our bearings and minds…it was not turkey season! We still took the bird home, a little nervous that a game warden would pull us over. That never happened and that turkey tasted just fine to us!

Nita Maxine-Lorena Stanley's Dairy Bar

"Whatever you do, work at it with all your heart, as working for the Lord, not for human masters, since you know you will receive an inheritance from the Lord as a reward. It is the Lord Christ you are serving." Colossians 3:23-24 (NIV)

Things were so different. Cliff couldn't work anymore. The heart attack took him down in a way that we never thought it would. He was disabled, my husband was disabled. I could not believe that because I was too young to deal with this. Linda and Barabara were older now and mostly out of the house, but we still had five of us in the house, five mouths to feed and clothe. It had taken years to get social security and the compensation for his lung disease, deemed black lung,

It's not like I really wanted to work, but maybe I did. It was a feeling I had never felt, at least for a long time. It was exhilarating, in a sense. There was a whole world outside of feeding and clothing seven people and running a home, albeit at Lorena Stanley's Dairy Bar. I had gotten the job to help out with the bills although Cliff wasn't excited about a mom working away from her children and family.

It wasn't a hard job, mostly running the cash register, handing out food and ice cream from the kitchen and talking to customers. Maybe that's the part I liked best, the talking part. Most interactions were short, unsubstantial. Yet, talking to the customers and people I knew from town made me realize I was more than a mom, doing the washing, cleaning and cooking. People asked how I was, how the kids were, how Cliff was getting along. It helped me to be a part of something outside of myself. It felt good.

I even got to work with my oldest daughter. It was probably hard for her, seeing her mom, sharing the same job as your mom when you were a young woman just entering the world. I tried not to invade her space, interfere with her work, and just give her the "professional space" she needed. It was fun to sit back and watch her interact with customers, work diligently at tasks, and wrap things up at the end of the day. We did not have many shifts together, but it was sort of a silent knowing when we were on the same shift, knowing we were both doing our best, helping. I even had peace about not knowing what would come next for us all.

Barbara-Not My Plan

> *"For I know the plans I have for you," declares the Lord,*
> *"plans to prosper you and not to harm you, plans to*
> *give you a hope and a future." Jeremiah 29:11 (NIV)*

I worked in a summer camp back in 1968. I remember one June day when I got the call that dad was sick. I will never forget the feeling of my very own heart sinking to my knees when I heard mom say, "He's had a heart attack. He's sick…"

The ride from Bob Jones University in South Carolina seemed even longer than it ever had been before. I came home to face my siblings, my mom and my dad. They were broken and sad and scared because the strong-willed man that ran our home was sick. Would he make it? What could the doctors do for him?

In the face of so much uncertainty, I decided to stay home. How could I leave everyone anyways? Wouldn't that seem selfish? What if I left and I never got to see my dad alive again?

So, there I stayed in Beckley, West Virginia. I decided to stay home, save my money, as I worked at the C & P Telephone Company until January of 1970. I decided to go to Marshall University at that point in January. I ended up graduating the next year in 1971.

This wasn't really my plan, but God's plans always seem to look different. I hadn't planned on the starting and stopping points, but they were necessary in making me who I would become. These stopping points are just intersections in our lives for God to show up.

I even got married on New Year's Eve in 1971 to Bill Welsh. Some parts of His plan were even better than I expected.

Nita Maxine-Golf at Grandview

"I have a tip that can take five strokes off anyone's game. It's called an eraser." Arnold Palmer

---

He was out in the garage, cleaning his golf clubs. Golfing at Grandview again, probably the fourth time this week. A part of me resented him for this. He golfed, I worked. But just as my heart started to turn cold at the edges, it melted. I realized the baggage I held onto was not the only baggage in this home. He had gone on with his life, he had created a new identity in which productivity was not the epicenter. He had taken his real estate test and received his realtor license and went on to help others buy their homes and sell property in the Beckley area.

There were hard times, days that were harder than others, times when I think we both wished for something different. Yet, we both picked up our baggage and moved along. The baggage of our pasts and presents often weighed us down, but it never stopped us, we kept going despite the odds against us. Could life have turned out differently? Yes. But this was our life, our gift from the Greatest Giver.

I smiled as I saw him putting his clubs away and walking into the house, that straw hat tilted slightly on his head, "Got anything to eat Max?" Life was a gift even on these normal days.

Nita Maxine-Gifts and Gloves

"Every good and perfect gift is from above, coming down from the Father of the heavenly lights, who does not change like the shifting shadows." James 1:17(NIV)

Having a December birthday is often a problem, mainly because when you're a kid, you get Christmas/ birthday gifts, not Christmas and birthday gifts.

I will never forget the look on Cliff's face as he opened his birthday gifts one by one that year, revealing not one but five pairs of gloves. He was older, the children all grown with kids of their own. Everyone could tell you just how Cliff would open his gifts, taking out his pocketknife and slowly making a slit at each end of the gift where the paper had been taped. This little birthday gift opening dance, if you will, would take sometimes five minutes just to open one gift. As Cliff would slowly and deliberately fold the paper for safe keeping, the crowd of birthday onlookers would breathe a sigh of relief.

So, after all of this opening, he had five pairs of gloves, they were all different types of gloves, but gloves. He finally looked up and asked, "Is this a joke?" He smiled and there was a slight twinkle in his eyes. I guess the kids knew this one thing, even without being able to work, their dad was always working, doing, and using his hands. From driving gloves to dress gloves to outdoor, heavy work gloves, their daddy's hands were still important and something to be protected, cherished, even as all five children were adults now.

We all laughed that night as we watched Cliff open gifts, his white hair combed down next to his bald head, his eyes still a startling blue in his old age. I still see a semblance of his youth on nights like this, the eyes that drew me in at sixteen and still catch me off guard today. I watched as Cliff joked with the kids and the grandkids, offering everyone a pair of gloves as if they needed one. We sang happy birthday and ate cake and watched the grandkids running around as our own kids tried to settle them down, reprimanding them for being too loud. It was life full circle. It was good, not perfect, but good.

JEFF-NIMROD

Cush was the father of Nimrod, who began to be a mighty one on the earth. He was a mighty hunter before the Lord; so it is said, "Like Nimrod, a mighty hunter before the Lord." Genesis 10:8-12

Later on, after Sandy and I were married, dad and I went hunting with her stepdad, Fin. Finley aka. Fin, had property in Streeter where he hunted and we decided to go out there one fall day. We took Lady, the rabbit hunting dog, with us and she immediately got to work.

We had set up around the power line where the grass was a bit shorter but perfect for rabbits. Lady kept her nose to the ground and started yipping once she saw a rabbit. As Lady is yipping, I look ahead of her and notice that a rabbit is about twenty yards ahead of her. Lady and I are deep in hunting mode while dad and Fin are talking back and forth, completely clueless to what is happening.

I turn around and tell them to look at Lady and that the rabbit is close. Fin laughs a big hearty laugh and tells me not to shoot because I won't be able to take the rabbit down from this far away.

If you know anything about me as a hunter, it's that I will always take the shot. This time was no exception and I shot straight toward the rabbit. Lady started trailing it and let us know that the rabbit was down.

Fin looked at me in surprise and shock, telling me he didn't think anyone could have gotten that rabbit. From then on Fin called me Nimrod, from the Bible, who was a great hunter and Noah's great grandson. I had never heard that name before that day.

Dad just stood there and smiled taking it all in. I wonder if dad was proud or laughing inside, thinking did Jeff's father-in-law just call him a Nimrod? I guess I'll never know but I do remember having a great day in the woods with my dad and a man who would become a great father figure to me.

Joan-Daddy

"A daughter has on open door into a father's heart."-
Abraham Verghese in "The Covenant of Water

I was so sick. I couldn't hold my head up. Everything was vivid, like a lucid dream. I couldn't stop throwing up and daddy held my hand and my head over the toilet. It wouldn't stop and the tears streamed down my face. I clung to daddy's neck and threw up over the back of his head. I have no idea how long it had been and how we got there but I woke up in a bed with a starched white sheet. Was I dying? Was I in heaven? I looked over and daddy smiled at me. I must have asked if I was dying. He simply said, "No Joanie. You'll be just fine." He turned his head and I think I saw tears caught in the corner of his eyes, but I still can't be sure to this day.

It's funny because I remember daddy in this tender way. Maybe by the time I came around, his role was different, being more of a caregiver in the home than just working to provide for us. Mom was going to school and eventually got her nursing degree and went back to work. She was busy, working to provide for us; my parents' roles had changed drastically but I knew the love they had for me hadn't

49

changed. I remember dad being there, telling me stories at night and tucking me in. Things were different by the time I was growing up with mom and dad. Different isn't always bad.

ANNALEE-JUST KEEP SWIMMING

*"My grandmother started walking five miles a day
when she was sixty. She's ninety-seven now, and we
don't know where the heck she is."- Ellen Degeneres*

I think my grandmother hoped to give us cultural experiences, maybe she never had or exposure to the world in ways she had hoped to have when she was young. She would take us to the Living Christmas Tree at Memorial Baptist Church in Beckley. She would take us to see the local performance of the Nutcracker when we were little and we would spend the evening trying not to laugh at the men in tights, and yet somehow being mesmerized by the costumes, displays, music and dancing.

One of my first memories of grandma was going with her to the Beckley YMCA. It was huge to me back then. As soon as you walked in the front door, you could smell the chlorine and hear the squeaks of tennis shoes as they moved around the basketball court.

I remember her swimming laps as we splashed around in the pool, usually it was my sister Angie and me. We were sometimes joined by our cousins Laura, Andrew and William but not that often. I really don't know how long she swam but it must have been hours each time we went, enough for all of our water games to start to feel old and boring and our fingers to become little prunes floating atop the water. My grandmother would just swim and swim with her swim cap on. She had ear problems so keeping the water out of them was imperative.

She glided over the water, one lap at a time. She never swam too fast or too slow. She just kept going and would glide to the end of a lane and sometimes touch it and turn her body. I remember seeing her do a flip turn one time, or maybe that was my imagination. At any rate, she was a decent swimmer and I remember thinking she must really like the water. I think she mainly loved exercise, moving forward at any rate. She would often go to the state park nearby, Little Beaver, to walk laps around the lake, walking miles at a time. I'm sure she did a lot of thinking and praying while she was out there. I'm sure she prayed a lot for me for my family.

She had endless energy. Every family member agreed about this and often laughed about how she would outlive us all and let us know all about it. I loved her energy. I miss her.

Jeff-Our Very Own Gypsies

"My soul is from elsewhere. I'm sure of that.
And I intend to end up there." Rumi

I slipped through the front door as quickly and quietly as I could. It had been a warm, fall day early in October and the moon was bright overhead. A breeze was floating through the trees as we kicked at rocks and made our way down to the L& B Supermarket, about a mile from our house.

We had seen them passing through for the past few days in their caravans. It was like something out of a movie, something from a wild world that we had never existed in. They had furniture and other goods that they made from wood and sold to people in our town. We felt like we were watching the most exotic, foreign people we could ever see in Beckley, West Virginia. We were watching real life gypsies. The girls were beautiful with their long hair and colorful clothing, like fairies floating through our town that would appear one day and be gone soon.

These people, who seemed to be transported from another world and time, lived amongst our very normal, regular community in Beckley, WV for a week or so out of the year. As if they were passing through to assess what they could and couldn't take from the community, houses that were otherwise left unlocked, were safely locked tight. Mothers held their children's hands a little tighter and fathers looked over their shoulders.

No matter how the community felt about these real life gypsies, I was so intrigued by them. It made me think about how other people lived, how they traveled and made a living, how their children went to school or maybe didn't. What a life!

My neighbor and I continued to kick at the rocks as we made our way toward the L & B, knowing we probably shouldn't be going but here we were, embarking on an exotic adventure-or so we felt. I smiled and whistled a tune that I was learning on my guitar. I knew we didn't have a lot of time but this was worth it.

We made our way past the L & B, where we could just make out the light of fire in the woods situated behind the supermarket. The smell of smoke and something that smelled a little like barbecue wafted through the air. We found a small crate behind the side of the supermarket and stood on our tiptoes to see through the trees that had now turned dark, like old spindly hands spreading their fingers to the sky.

As if on cue, someone started singing a song we had never heard, a guitar strumming along caught the melody and a tambourine held onto the beat. A few of the colorfully dressed women seemed to float up along with the music as they danced and sang. It was one of the most beautiful and strange sights I had ever encountered, right here behind the supermarket where my mom bought our food.

We noticed some smaller children joining into the dance, walking, and dancing around the fire with the women and a few men. Their makeshift tents were set up near the fire. I wondered how long they would be here and if the children had to be at school soon. Where did they bathe and where did they keep their food? My young mind raced with questions.

We watched for what seemed like a long time, through a few songs and dances, and we even tapped our own feet to the strange, tribal beat. We knew we had to get back and didn't want to be seen by the gypsies or our parents out here on this old crate, spying like young boys do. We climbed off the crates, making our way home, talking about what it would be like to travel the country like the gypsies and never have to go to school. We whistled a gypsy tune the rest of the way home.

Joan—Summer Carnivals

"She wanted none of those days to end and it was always
with disappointment that she watched the darkness
stride forward." Markus Zusak, The Book Thief

Summer had officially begun. Days were longer and hotter and everyone was always outside. Maybe it was because our parents made us stay outside or that's just what we were expected to do back then. There was no video game or television competing for our time back then. Only programs that came on at certain hours of the evening-and we were back home by then for the most part. The woods outside of our house were like a retreat that called to us daily. A world run by kids that parents would never understand where there was a hierarchy of neighborhood children dictating who got to swing on the largest trees and decide what game we played next.

Riding from the house to the corner where the woods opened up behind Pinecrest Hospital seemed like a long ride at times. Now I realize it was well less than a mile and must have taken a matter of minutes on a bike. That's how it was though, getting somewhere as a kid seemed to take forever and then when you were there, the time slipped so quickly like sand through your fingers. The next thing you knew your mom was calling for you or you noticed the streetlights flickering overhead.

One hot July day, we noticed a truck pulling up behind the Pinecrest Hospital. It was colorful and out of place in our very normal surroundings. The truck was printed with the name of a traveling carnival. It was time. The carnival was back. We gathered our friends to watch the carnival people erecting the rides and buildings that would house the games that we would beg our parents for loose change in exchange to get to play them. Maybe we would even win a prize- a goldfish or a stuffed teddy bear. To walk home with a prize from the local carnival was like walking home after you had been crowned royalty-the princess of Hedrick Street, I would feel like. I would probably display a prize like that for several months in my room, making sure everyone knew I had won it by tossing a penny into a jug or popping a balloon with a dart. That's what the carnival did for me, it made me dream.

I even dreamed of the large Ferris wheel climbing high into the sky, touching the clouds and the green, high hills of Beckley. I would ride on the Ferris wheel with my best of friends. We would all show up in matching bows and dresses and everyone would "ooh and awe" at the cutest girls they had ever seen giggling and munching cotton candy as they climbed ever higher and higher.

We watched the carnival people as they built and sweat and swore and smoked and laughed. I wondered how a person would get a job like this and what qualifications they would need. They were an interesting breed-broad shouldered and tan men looking in need of a good shave and shower; women who were overly painted and ornately dressed to catch your eye as you passed to guess the weight of the fat woman or entice you to hit a bell with a large rubber mallet to see just how strong you really were.

These people had seen the world, or at least the country. I often wondered where they like to stay the best or if the thought ever occurred to them.

As I watched the carnival being built in the large field behind the armory and then later being torn down, I would think about the cotton candy, the rides and the people-always the people. Where would they go next? Would they miss this place?

Nita Maxine-New Cars
and Negotiations

"A penny saved is a penny earned." Benjamin Franklin

It was time for a new car for Joan. She was in need of new transportation, and I had agreed to go to the Subaru dealership with her. Even as I agreed, my mind reeled with the thoughts of having to deal with salesmen, being pushy and loud and making me feel inferior in some way if I didn't choose their vehicle. I really loathed this type of thing but as I dressed smartly in a pants suit and grabbed my purse, I pasted a smile on my face that told Joan otherwise.

We made the drive to Narrows, Virginia where Joan was set on finding a new Subaru. She had joked and said that if she didn't find a deal there, we might be walking home since she wasn't sure her old car would make it back up I-77 past Camp Creek.

It was a large car lot with hundreds of vehicles but when Joan settled on the one she liked, she went back and forth with the salesman. After much thought and deciding he was not going to give her the financial incentives for buying the car that she needed, she shook his hand politely and said this was not the time to buy the car. It was a polite transaction but for some reason, I could not bring myself to move. I knew that in the kosher manner of business transactions, now would be the time to move my rear, extend my hand and thank the salesman for helping my daughter. I couldn't though. I thought of walking up that mountain and I will say that I think I got misty eyed. That would nearly kill us and Joan needed this car.

As I was just about to stand up and leave with Joan, the salesman took in my young daughter escorted by her fretting mother-it must have been on my face- and he told Joan he would give her the deal she had wanted. We left that day with a new car from the Subaru dealership in Narrows and we did not have to walk up the mountain near Camp Creek.

I laughed as we drove away from the dealership and Joan started laughing too. We both agreed the car ride up the mountain trumped any walking we would have done.

Barbara-Time Stands Still at Marshall University

"In the middle of Huntington, West Virginia there's a river. Next to this river there is a steel mill. And next to this steel mill there is a school. In the middle of the school, there is a fountain. Each year on the exact same day, at the exact same hour, the water to this fountain is turned off. And at this moment once every year, throughout the town, throughout the school, time stands still." opening line,
"We are Marshall" the movie

"We are…Marshall!"-every MU student

I ended up going back to Marshall University in Huntington, West Virginia. I was about to start school the upcoming semester after saving money from my job at the phone company. It was November 14, 1970. I was about to head home for Thanksgiving.

I will never forget the news that evening. It was like time had stopped. Everyone was sad. Everyone cried-even if you had no idea who the people in the plane really were-even if you really didn't know them. You still felt a connection to the tragedy, to the loss that connected a small steel mill community, in southern West Virginia. You could almost feel the loss as if your own brother or father or son had died.

The Marshall University football team was on their way to East Carolina University on a private chartered plane. The weather was rainy and dark. It was around eight in the evening when the plane crashed. The entire team, coaches and a few fans were killed- seventy-five people. It was tragic.

I had never seen a loss that huge. I didn't understand it. How could a group of people be here one minute and be gone the next? But that's how it was. Sudden loss. A tragedy I would never really get over. It changed the community in Huntington too. It became "before the crash" and "after the crash" when people would discuss local events.

I remember finals being suspended that year, students were allowed to leave and grieve and be with their families. So that is what they did. We left and I went back to Beckley. I hugged my sisters and brothers tightly and I looked a little more intently at my parents, trying to memorize their every move because you never know what could happen next.

LINDA-RAILROAD TRACKS AND METAL DETECTORS

---

*"Kind words are like honey-sweet to the soul and
healthy for the body." Proverbs 16:24 (NLT)*

I had been away for a while studying and then after that, using my nursing degree. I think dad was tired and needed a break from everything so when I arrived back home, after a few hours, he asked me if I would want to go try out his new metal detector. I reluctantly said yes. I was tired and honestly didn't feel up for adventures, but it wasn't very often that dad asked.

We ended up in Fitzpatrick, walking near the railroad tracks, near where we all used to swim when we were kids-we had called our swimming place, "The Blue Hole". Dad ended up heaving his metal detector along as we made our way down the tracks. I'm not sure what treasures he would find along this track but he brought it anyway. Sometimes dad got in these moods where he just wanted to talk. Today was one of those days.

He talked and I listened. He told me about what he had been doing at home while I was gone, we talked about the street and the neighborhood, who had come and gone. He talked about his time in the war briefly as we noticed a plane overhead. He said he had never been afraid of heights until after the war, after he had been a rear gunner in World War II. He had been on twenty-six missions. Most men barely made it out of one or two missions alive. He had once been on a mission where they had counted twenty-one holes in the B-17 he flew after he had landed. He talked about how he would look over and be so close to the other planes that he could make out the faces of the other gunners and pilots. He didn't say it exactly, but I know it made him sad. As he reflected and remembered, he got a distant look in his eyes. I wonder if he was thinking about a specific person he had seen or a specific mission.

War was a hard thing he had told me. He never really talked about war with anyone, this was a rare occasion. I soaked up the day, the breeze, the sunshine hitting us as we walked along the tracks. I smiled briefly as dad grabbed my hand and held it for a minute, seeing a completely different side of him. I appreciated this moment with him. It was mine alone.

DAVID-CHRISTMAS CANDY MONEY

"In the cookies of life, siblings are the chocolate chips." Mario Puzo, The Godfather (1969)

Shopping near Christmas time was always fun, although hard not to want everything you saw in the windows. I remember loading up the car one Monday night since the stores were open longer near the Christmas holiday. Jeff was on crutches, and it took painfully longer for everyone to get in the car and settled around the wooden crutches. The crutches had become a permanent fixture for us all since Jeff had to use them for a few months. He had a growing disease called Osgood Schlatter's, where he grew faster than his muscles could keep up with. Really it just meant more time dodging another weapon my older brother could use against me. These crutches and new weaponry took up residence now between my face and the back seat window, leaning against Jeff but somehow more on my side than his anyways.

We drove as Christmas carols played in the background from the local radio station. I was staring at the holiday lights, and everything all decked out for Christmas as we arrived in uptown Beckley to finish our last-minute holiday shopping. I was used to tagging along with everyone, being the youngest, and I was happy to be paired up with Jeff for our holiday excursion.

We followed our parents through several stores and the novelty of the shopping experience seemed to get old pretty fast, especially when everything looked so bright and new and shiny, but you were told that you would just "have to wait until Christmas and see what Santa brought". Mom went into Murphy's and told us we could go along with her, but we were tired of trailing behind her and being told we couldn't buy our own toys and things. Jeff and I opted to sit outside and do some people watching. We would most likely see people we knew or at least witness some interesting "uptown" behavior.

We were sitting on a bench, Jeff's crutches leaned up against the back of it. We were talking about how much candy we thought we could eat before we would throw up, basic kid conversation, when a well-dressed man in a suit and tie walked up to us. Maybe we looked bored or sad or abandoned. I'm not sure which but the man looked Jeff square in the eyes and asked him about his crutches. Jeff looked up with a sad look and mentioned that he had just been diagnosed with a disease and he had to have the crutches now. The man in the fancy suit looked suddenly sad and taken aback. He handed us some money and wished us well and told us to have a Merry Christmas.

As soon as he was out of ear shot, we could not control the laughter bubbling up in our throats. I also could not believe our luck. I guess the man in the fancy suit, maybe a preacher or something, had thought Jeff's disease was fatal and a few dollars would contribute to his cure.

Either way, we strode through the front doors of Murphy's and straight to the candy section. Maybe we would have a chance to see how much candy it would take for us to get sick.

NITA MAXINE-TAKE MY SEAT

"You have not lived today until you have done something for someone who can never repay you." John Bunyan

---

I was exhausted. Honestly, I had been tired for the past fifteen plus years so today was really no different. I was on my way out to run some errands after the kids had gotten off to school that day. There were bills to be paid, groceries to pick up; life did not stop just because I needed a break.

David had one more year before he would start kindergarten, so he became my little sidekick each day. He would watch Captain Kangaroo and ask about where his sister Joanie was, while I washed and folded clothes or did whatever other chores needed done. In a house with seven people, there was laundry most daily, things to be scrubbed and straightened before it all started all over again the next day.

We walked to the bus stop near Pinecrest to catch the bus to town. I held tightly to David's hand as he had just taken a spell of wandering off lately whenever he saw something new and interesting. I was seriously too tired to have to do my regular daily chores plus find a missing child.

We walked up the steps of the bus and found our seats. We watched as the houses and businesses passed by and David sweetly asked, "How long will this bus ride be mommy?" I told him not too long and we stared ahead as the bus driver stopped at another stop not too far from our own. A young African American lady sauntered onto the bus with a bulging belly. The bus was full by this time, and everyone seemed to be too absorbed in their own daily activities or maybe didn't notice her. I couldn't believe that everyone was ignoring her, and she even asked a man who was sitting near the front if she could sit down, and he only shook his head no and grunted in response.

The audacity of the people on the bus hit a nerve. I knew how this lady felt, tired, maybe she was on her way to run the same errands I was running, maybe she was returning from a long shift or going to work for the day. Either way, I looked at David and said, "We have to move." He looked wide-eyed and just grabbed my hand. We stood up and walked near the back of the bus and held onto a large metal pole near the back seats. I motioned for the lady to sit in our seat. She smiled and quickly thanked me.

I was tired that day, but I think maybe the good Lord sent that lady my way to remind me that there is always someone out there that you can be kind to, even if you are bone tired and think you have absolutely nothing to give.

Grandma Scarborough (Elvira) -Aprons and Paring Knives

"One of the few articles of clothing that a man won't try to remove from a woman is an apron." Marilyn Vos Savant

---

I looked through the back window and noticed I could hear the kids playing in the side yard. This was a favorite pastime for them, and for many of the neighborhood children. A quick glance at the kitchen clock and I saw that it was nearing 3:30 in the afternoon. Usually, Nita would try to have a quick afternoon nap by this time and be working on the evening's dinner.

I had grown to love living beside Clifford and Nita and all the kids. Sure, sometimes it felt cramped and I had to wonder if Ted and Marie would have liked me to leave but this was family and this is what we did-we took care of one another.

I smiled and grabbed my apron. I remembered Nita saying she had just got some nice apples and would need to cut them. I know one thing for sure, a woman could always find something to do but it was much more palatable if you had good company to share the workload.

I walked over and waved at the kids playing in the side yard, close now to getting in a fight over who had won the baseball game. Although they knew not to fight, or Cliff and Nita would send them all home and their own kids to their rooms. I had to chuckle at that sometimes. They were doing a good job raising a family though and I was proud of them.

As I walked through the door I could smell chicken baking in the oven, and I noticed green beans in a pot. "Need some help Nita?" I asked her as I gave her a quick side hug and sat down. She wiped her hair out of her eyes and pointed to the apples she had just got. "I did get a bushel of apples and I need to cut some for applesauce for dinner tonight."

Before she even finished her thoughts, I was bending over to pull out a few apples and sitting them down on my lap. I pulled an old paring knife out of my apron pocket and started cutting and peeling apples. Nita looked over at me and smiled, sighed, and thanked me. I just gave a little laugh. She knew she never had to thank me, but she did, always, that was her disposition.

I loved being close to the kids, the constant chaos and commotion, the movement of everyday family life. I sat back each day and said a silent prayer for each of my children and grandchildren and family members. Just being here was blessing enough.

David-Don't be Late for Dinner

---

*"I don't care what they call me, so long as they don't
call me late for dinner."* Frederick Marryat

Dinner was served promptly between 4:30 and 5:00 daily. This was just how things were. It was the way that my mom and dad liked our household to be run and it was all that we knew.

One cool, crisp fall day, we had a good game of kickball going on in the side yard. My team was up by two runs, and I was feeling pretty good about our luck. I was usually put on the team that was composed of the younger kids, the brothers or sisters or cousins that were always told what to do because of their line in the pecking order. Today was a good day for winning despite my team and our overall odds.

I remember going up to the home plate as Jeff rolled the ball out to me to kick. I kicked it far left and was able to round all the way to third base before the ball was thrown back to the catcher. I exhaled sharply and called out to Jeff and the others about how we were going to kick their butts this time.

Just as I had settled my left foot into the base and had poised myself to run straight home, I heard the back door open and mom yell that it was dinner time. I could hardly believe my luck. Here I was, about to hit home plate and make the winning run and it was already dinner time. Jeff snickered and walked off the kicking area and muttered something about "better luck next time". I screamed to the top of my lungs, "We still won!" Even as I screamed the older kids laughed and turned to say their good-bye's knowing it was probably almost time for their dinner too.

I see the value in a nightly dinner around the table with everyone there. I definitely see it now, as I have my own family but then, I didn't see the point at all. I barely touched my food that night and I'm pretty sure I "accidentally" kicked Jeff under the table.

Nita Maxine-On Growing Up

---

*"Life would be infinitely happier if we could
only be born at the age of eighty and gradually
approach eighteen."* Mark Twain

The house was a wreck. We had been remodeling for
what seemed like ages. The kids were still there, along with
Cliff and I. It wasn't like we could afford to go stay in a hotel
while all the repairs were being completed but some days,
that is exactly what I wished for.

Linda came home one day after school, asking excitedly
about having a friend stop by that weekend. I said yes, of
course, if they didn't mind the mess. Linda was so excited
and immediately ran from the room.

A couple of days later, I heard a knock on the door and
Linda opened it to greet her school friend. Linda was excited
and the girl answered her kindly. After a few moments of
walking around the house, I heard the girl ask, "Are you
poor or something?" I heard Linda laugh it off and say we
were remodeling.

It was the first time as a mom that I wanted to intervene
and go tell that little girl that she had no manners and it
was impolite to ask certain questions, that no, we were not

poor but worked extremely hard for everything we had and we were remodeling to provide space for our large family. In my mind I chased the girl out the front door as she cried and apologized the entire way out the door. Linda and I sat on the front stoop and waved at her.

Alas, I did not intervene nor chase the girl out of our home, although my blood boiled. It would not be the first time I would hear my children be the brunt of rude behavior or feel like I needed to run to their aid. I didn't this time. Linda was a teenager, she didn't need my help and it would only create more problems. A part of my heart was sad and I remembered those snide remarks that little girls often make about this or that, even when I was growing up.

Linda hugged me after her friend left that day. I hugged her tightly and marked the feeling in my bank of memories. Linda was getting older and was so independent, she often overlooked a hug or embrace so for her to initiate was a treasure to me. I am not sure if she was feeling sad or just the way you feel after you realize even some friends aren't perfect, they will rip little pieces of your heart away if you let them. Growing up and growing old is a hard thing to do. It is not for the faint of heart.

BARBARA-HERE WE GO!

"Travel makes one modest. You see what a tiny place you occupy in the world." Gustave Flaubert

---

Mom loved to travel as she got older and after dad died. I think it was because she never did get the opportunity to do so as she was growing up. I mean the furthest she had traveled was Charleston, West Virginia and then to El Paso, Texas when she was sixteen to marry dad.

To celebrate mom's 70th birthday, I decided it would be a lovely time to take a trip to visit some New England states and to do some leaf peeping. Mom was a pretty good traveler-as long as she got a good night's rest and was fed properly along the way. We went to so many places that will remain in my memories: Lexington and Concord, Walden Pond, Boston Harbor, Old North Church, and Paul Revere's house. We looked at beautiful mansions along the bluff shores in Newport, Rhode Island. Mom always complained of the fishy smell at the fishing ports which made me chuckle each time. This could have been one of the reasons she declined to eat any lobster when we were on our trip.

Mom was a fan of LL Bean clothing and we got to visit the original store while we were in Maine. In New Hampshire, we saw the Old Man of the Mountain on Cannon Mountain. It collapsed in 2003 so I guess it was lucky that we did see that. New England was full of surprises from the ports to cranberry bogs to the historical sites and sweeping views of the fall leaves. I think that was a trip that mom remembered fondly.

She traveled more with us as a family, on family vacations to Canaan Valley, Blackwater Falls and Sunset Beach. She traveled on a bus with me and Laura to New York City and even later went to New Orleans to visit Rita and Don.

Mom's step was a little lighter as she aged. Maybe it was the worries of caring for five children and a husband that had always made her so serious. Maybe it was releasing us all to our own lives and families, she was more joyful and smiled more easily. She was always up for a road trip, to see something new, to take on a new adventure-we just had to make sure we had snacks on hand.

NITA MAXINE-FAITHFUL

---

*"For God so loved the world that He gave His
one and only Son, that whoever believes in Him
will have eternal life." John 3:16 (NIV)*

I had heard about Jesus and church all my life. Growing
up in the Bible belt, I am pretty sure everyone did hear about
such things. I had always been a good person, kept my nose
clean so to speak, and just worked hard with the things and
the responsibilities thrown my way.

From a young age, I had to help cook and clean and
take care of the household chores. I had to have dinner on
the table and clean up before most kids even realized how
to boil water. Mom had been sick and when she died at
forty-one, I had the responsibility of a mom to an extent. I
think I took that seriously. I knew it was important. I had
a sister to take care of and sometimes, even my dad. It was
a lot for a young girl, but I never knew anything different.
I knew God was present in my life but honestly, I was too
busy as I grew up, too busy trying and doing and being for
everyone else to really look at my faith and think about what
that meant in my life.

I had been to church as a kid and most of my family had ties to churches and to God and to faith. It wasn't until I was older though that I realized my desire to profess my need for Jesus and to ask Him to be a part of my life. It was 1964, I had teenage daughters and a preteen son with two more climbing the ranks. I needed to establish a church home for my family. I realized that even though I hadn't been a part of a church body for a long time, if truly ever, I had a faith in God that caused me to pray when things got hard, praise when things were good and to look at the beauty of creation in awe knowing it was created with heavenly hands.

I had taken the kids to church services at Regular Baptist Church and they had attended vacation Bible school every summer. That was important to me. Cliff was different. He was working out his own faith, his own salvation, and as hard as it was to go to church alone with the kids, I became accustomed to it. So one Sunday, as an altar call was given, I went to the front of the church and told the pastor I wanted to dedicate my life to the Lord, to His service and that I wanted Him to be the Lord of my life. It was pretty simple. I prayed the sinner's prayer from the book of Romans in the Bible. I went home and not much had changed. Not much but my heart.

I would like to think I had a little more patience and grace with the kids and Cliff. Maybe some days I didn't. I tried. Every morning, I would read my Bible and pray, often leaving the Bible open on a table to come back to at quick moments in the day when I could. I think the Lord created a desire to learn about Him through His word in my heart. I hoped that would be my heart's desire to the end.

ANGIE-STIR IT UP, PLEASE!

"Your love is better than ice cream..." Sarah McLachlan

I climbed up onto the barstool. The stools had wooden slats and swiveled around so when you climbed on them, you felt important like a princess and could have fun all at the same time. Sometimes when no one was looking, I would swivel the bar stool completely around in full circles, almost making myself dizzy. When you got off the bar stools, you would have lines running down your legs, especially if you wore shorts or a dress. When it was hot, your legs would even stick on the seats.

You could see all the "up high" grown up things from the stools, like my grandparents' mail stack in the holder beside the rotary wall phone and the lamp that stretched from the wall over the bar counter. You could see the big letter opener that grandpa used to open letters, which honestly looked more like a weapon but I don't think he really liked to rip paper, even envelopes. You could even see my grandpa's magnifying glass up here. This was mainly off limits to the kids but we sometimes got to hold it if he was looking at something up close and we happened to be around.

Grandma had said it was time for dessert. We had eaten dinner and grandma had made pork and broccoli with orange runny cheese. I never tried that because the smell made me gag. I think she thought if she put cheese on it, we would try it. At least she had good intentions.

Anyways, dessert time was always a treat. Grandma would pull out the plastic Tupperware bowls in orange, green and yellow. She would expertly scoop ice cream with an actual ice cream scoop. I'm pretty sure we just used spoons at our house. It was like watching an artist in their element. After the big, fat white scoops had hit the bowl, grandma would always ask if I wanted syrup, chocolate syrup. Sometimes she might have strawberry or even some of the ice cream crackle coating but I always got the chocolate.

After a heaping helping of syrup, I dug in but not until grandma also sat down beside me with her own bowl of ice cream. She would smile and stir her own ice cream into an ice cream smoothie in a bowl. It was magical and delicious. She would always ask me if I wanted my ice cream stirred and of course I always said yes. This was the magic of grandma's ice cream.

To this day, I would rather stir my ice cream, no matter the flavor, syrup or no syrup. There is something not only nostalgic but absolutely delicious and comforting about a bowl of smooth, creamy, stirred ice cream.

LINDA-CIGARETTES AND LAUGHS

---

*"Life is worth living as long as there's a
laugh in it."* L.M. Montgomery

I remember the smell of the smoke more than really seeing daddy ever smoke cigarettes. Back then, smoking a cigarette was like having a glass of tea on a hot summer day, it was just something people did. It was social and highly acceptable.

I was walking through the backyard one day when I saw a perfect little yellow stub of a cigarette butt. It still had a little of the white on it. I picked it up and put it between my fingers like I had seen dad do about a thousand times. I pretended to be a movie star as I "inhaled and exhaled" the cigarette. I even began to talk to my costars in a dreamy Hollywood voice. "You look marvelous darling." I rolled my eyes back in my head and smiled as I pretended to be "Linda the Great", with beautiful curls and red lipstick and pretty ball gown.

The only thing was, when I looked back down at the ground and up again, I saw dad standing there. He looked at me and said, "Get that blasted thing out of your mouth Linda." I immediately ran away from dad, expecting a full-on spanking for putting that dirty old cigarette butt in my mouth.

I ran to the left and dad ran to the right. I flew on wings as I made the turn around the first corner. I'm not sure what I thought I was actually doing, or where I was going, I mean, I guess he would have had to eventually find me no matter how quickly I ran. As I rounded the last corner to the backyard, dad was going the other way and we collided straight into each other with such gusto, I almost had the wind knocked from my lungs. I tensed and readied myself for the discipline that would soon entail this meeting.

The funniest thing happened though; dad started to laugh. He laughed so hard he had tears forming in the corner of his eyes. When I realized how silly we must have looked, each of us running from one side of the house to the other, I started to giggle too. We both laughed and giggled so hard that day and I never picked up another cigarette, butt or whole, the rest of my life.

Nita Maxine-Sweet Treats

"We are all more blind to what we have than to what we have not." Audre Lorde

It wasn't much but I knew they enjoyed it. It was the littlest of things that could make a crew of five children happy. This littlest of life's enjoyments was fudge. Plain old chocolate fudge. They loved it and gobbled it like it was the last morsel of food they would ever eat. I secretly loved every moment of it, the excitement of seeing the small cubes of fudge sitting on the oval plate, just waiting for them. The "thank you's" and "Love you mom" that trailed along after they got their share.

Let's face it, I couldn't give my kids a lot. I knew that. Even before the world got smaller with telephones and computers, there was still that ugly thing called comparison that creeped in, threatening to ruin the best of days. I wanted to give my kids everything, but it was not possible. They were happy enough, I knew that. They played and loved to be with family and friends and cousins. They ran around the neighborhood playing, they were able to take piano and dance lessons, really for them, they were okay. They knew we didn't have much, but we had sure learned to stretch a penny, make clothes that would last and dinners from only a few ingredients. They were okay but as always, with most things, it's us parents who get it all confused and wrong, thinking we need to give our kids more things, more time, more of ourselves, more lessons, more food, simply more. I sometimes let that old ugly voice of comparison creep in, telling me my kids needed "more".

So the one way I would swipe that ugly voice away was to make what I could, with what I had. I stayed busy to a fault, I knew that I always had, but if I hadn't stayed busy my fear was that the house might go to shambles, yet another lie.

I would take what we had, look at the back of the old marshmallow fluff jar and I would make a grand tray of fudge, even buttering the tray to make sure the fudge didn't stick, leaving the slightest bit of salty creamy buttery flavor as you bit into the sweet chocolate fudge. It wasn't much but it was how I told that ugly voice to be quiet, how I calmed my nerves and made a few precious smiles in between.

JOAN-THE FIRST HEART ATTACK

"God is our refuge and strength,
an ever-present help in trouble.
² Therefore we will not fear, though the earth give way
and the mountains fall into the heart of the sea,
³ though its waters roar and foam
and the mountains quake with their surging"
Psalm 46:1-3 (NIV)

I remember being at the Little League field watching David play baseball. It was a pretty typical day. I enjoyed seeing my friends and neighbors at the field, catching up sometimes as I walked around and said hello to those I knew. Even though watching baseball could be boring at times, I had grown to enjoy watching my little brother and his team. They weren't the best team in the league but they weren't bad. I was learning more about the game and it was also something we did as a family. It was just me, David, and Jeff at the house now and mostly Jeff worked and came in and out a lot. It was like me, mom, dad and David were our own little family at times like this when we went to the field.

I had been sitting beside Daddy when he suddenly got up and said he needed to go to the truck to grab something. We figured he was heading out to grab his cigarettes or just take a break from sitting. He was gone for what seemed like forever and I told mom that. She looked at me and told me to go check on him if I was worried and she would stay there and continue watching the game.

I walked out to the truck, where I didn't see my dad sitting in the truck or standing beside. I thought that was strange, so I walked to the truck to peer inside. I was absolutely horrified to see daddy face down in the front cab of the truck. I opened the door and quickly asked him what was wrong. Was he ok? He weakly replied that he wasn't feeling well and had come out to "rest". I knew better than to shake my head and just take this explanation so I told him I would be right back. I ran back to tell mom and we ran back to the truck.

Mom drove us home, and a neighbor brought David back after his game. We got dad in the house, and he staggered inside to the old beige couch we used to have in the living room and fell face down again on the couch. He told mom she had better call an ambulance. I think she probably already was but at that time, there wasn't an ambulance service like we have today. Back then, you had to call a local funeral home and they had trucks that would pick you up to transport you to the local hospital.

It felt like forever, but they finally came to get daddy and they had only sent one man to help us. We couldn't lift him as he was dead weight at that point. I think mom called the neighbor boys and they helped the driver get daddy into the truck and to the hospital. I wasn't allowed to go and I needed to stay at home and wait for David anyways. I was in the eighth grade and that was when a lot of things in our house changed. I don't think I realized how different life would be once daddy came back after that first heart attack.

Nita Maxine-Broken Bones

"Your eyes saw my unformed body; all the days ordained for me were written in Your book before one of them came to be." Psalm 139: 16 (NIV)

It's the call you never want to receive, the knock on the door that you never want to hear. I had been cleaning up and Mr. Loyd Cox knocked on the door. I wasn't expecting a call at this hour, so I knew immediately something was not right. As Loyd stuttered and stammered his way through the story, I could feel myself go lightheaded.

This was not happening. As a coal miner's wife, you hear about tragic accidents leaving widows to care for children. As your husband leaves for work every morning, you pack their lunch tins with a prayer and a deeper appreciation that time is precious. I had always hated Cliff working in the coal mines, but it was West Virginia and coal mining was a booming industry and we had mouths to feed.

"Loyd, is he okay? Is he ALIVE?!" I couldn't take it anymore. I knew Loyd was doing his best but my heart was about to explode in my chest and my kids were about to find their mother passed out on the threshold of our tiny home if I didn't get a clear answer soon. After a few more misspoken words and stutters, Loyd was able to convey that Cliff was alive but badly injured.

The exhale that escaped my chest was audible and almost like a wheeze. I let out a small cry and then was able to get more details about where they were taking Cliff to be treated for a broken pelvis and a broken ankle.

As I greeted him in the hospital, sitting up in bed, looking weary and in pain, I was never so thankful for broken bones.

Jeff-The Sandbar

"So I decided there was nothing better than to enjoy food and drink and to find satisfaction in work. Then I realized that this pleasure is from the hand of God." Ecclesiastes 2:24-25 (NLT)

It was a Sunday afternoon and we had packed up a big lunch in the cooler. It was a gorgeous day, like a bluebird day with no clouds in the sky, perfect for swimming.

We loaded up to meet Uncle Woody, Aunt Elizabeth and all the kids. These days were the best. We headed to Prince, WV. We always went to the New River at the Sandbar. This was a perfect area for the kids to swim and run around, while the parents would sit out on blankets, talking and gossiping about the latest family and neighborhood news.

The Sandbar on the New River was a magical place for us. It was probably like going to the beach if you lived near the ocean, but I think it was better than that really. We would sit under shade trees, the river was cool and swift at times but never too harsh near this area. We didn't have to worry about waves like you did if you went to a beach near the ocean.

We pretended to be pirates and we would dive into the swimming hole for treasures, mainly coming out with rocks and clumps of grass.

There was something about coming down to this spot. It was like time stood still as everyone slowed down and sat along the beach, swam in the river and played games. Learning to swim here was also one of the greatest memories I have. I think that the sandbar was like a magical place for us all.

Nita Maxine-Just a quick nap

"Then Jesus said, Come to me, all of you who
are weary and carry heavy burdens, and I will
give you rest." Matthew 11:28 (NLT)

I was washing dishes. The day was hot, and I was standing near the kitchen window, praying for a breeze. I wiped my forehead with the back of my hand trying to keep the sweat from running into my eyes. I surveyed the backyard. As it stood, we had a fairly decent size garden, a few trees spread sporadically and as we often brought in farm animals for food. We currently had a pig, which to my chagrin, Jeff had named "Suzy". It was probably not best to name the animals that would one day become your food.

As I looked again at the back yard, I noticed a small mound lying beside the banana cherry tree. I hadn't seen Jeff and the other kids for a while and assumed they were down at the corner lot playing with cousins and friends. They would be back for dinner at least.

I approached the back door and looked more closely, squinting my eyes and sure enough I could make out Jeff laying under the tree, but he wasn't alone. Lying beside Jeff was another little mound, and this mound was snoozing just as sound as Jeff. Suzy was lying right beside Jeff.

I walked out the door without letting it slam behind me. I quietly approached the two peaceful nappers. It may have been one of the sweetest things I had ever seen. Jeff, with his arm draped over the round belly of that silly pig, the very pig we had told him not to get attached to. I heard Jeff breathe out as the pig grunted slightly in her sleep beside him. As much as I knew he shouldn't be doing this, I made a mental note to remember this moment in the back of my mind.

I bent over and slowly nudged Jeff to wake him up. As I did, he realized where he was and who was curled up beside him and he smiled up at me with a smile I won't soon forget. "Time for you and Suzy to wake up." He slowly stretched and stood up as Suzy trotted along behind him toward the house. What a pair.

NITA MAXINE-TIME FOR SCHOOL

"There is a time for everything, a season for every activity under heaven." Ecclesiastes 3:1 (NIV)

It was fall time again. After Labor Day, all the kids would go back to school. The ease of summer days would soon turn into more chaotic rhythms of school time. The summers were always peaceful at home, even with kids coming and going, doors slamming.

Linda and Barbara were excited for the start of a new year. We were blessed that both girls did well in school and cared about their grades. They studied when they had to and asked their teachers questions when they didn't understand things. Cliff and I always seemed to have good conferences with each of their teachers, both well-liked by peers and hard workers.

This year both girls would ride the bus to and from school. Jeff was not quite old enough to go to school yet but how he wished that he could follow his big sisters to this magical world that waited for them after they hopped on that big yellow bus. Jeff was the one I was most worried about. Even as a toddler, he loved to talk. I just hoped he would be able to listen to his teachers.

The last week of summer had come and gone and here we were getting ready for school. There was never enough space in our small bathroom but somehow the girls and everyone else managed, especially when we had to be at the bus stop on time.

Jeff had been mopey and sad the day before about the girls "leaving him". I told him his turn would soon come around to ride the yellow bus and learn new things at school. He didn't really care about what I said. He didn't throw tantrums, but he was plain old sad.

I really had no idea what to do but after talking to Cliff about it, it came to me. "How about we get you a lunch pail like the girls have?" He nodded his head and told me, "That's a good idea mom." I continued, "I will pack the very same lunch that the girls will have for that day, and you can eat it whenever you want and think about them and their day. You can walk with us to the bus and watch them leave for school in the morning and come home in the afternoon." I looked into his big eyes. "How's that sound?" To my surprise, it worked. Jeff smiled and told me he would love to eat what the girls ate and see the bus. I had done it. Crisis averted.

That first morning of school, Barbara and Linda walked ahead of us in their new outfits that I had made from a new fabric ream I had bought at the Piece Goods store. I thought that they looked rather smart in their new clothes. Even Jeff mentioned that they did look fancy today. I just hoped their first day would match their smart, new outfits.

I held Jeff's hand as Barbara and Linda climbed into the bus walked halfway to the back, and sat down. We waved as they peered out the window and smiled at us. Jeff even saluted them with his lunch pail. As we walked back to the house, Jeff settled himself on the stoop and pulled out his peanut butter sandwich. I asked him if he didn't want to wait to eat his sandwich for lunch to which he replied, "No mom, my brain is growing now, and I need food." I laughed at his silly remark, and this is how we proceeded for the rest of the school year.

Nita Maxine-Jelly Jars

"A sibling is the one person you rely on, fight with, and love unconditionally." Karen White, The Sound of Glass (2015)

I stored the jelly jars in a neat row under the cabinet nearest the sink. I would make jelly and store other things from our garden in the old jars to ensure we would have plenty to eat throughout the year. I had been working around the house, both girls had been out at school that day. It was just about time for them to come home. I needed to round Jeff up to go to the bus stop, but I couldn't find him anywhere. Mostly he was easy to find because he liked to talk so much, you could always hear him but not today. I figured he had curled up in a corner of a room and fallen asleep.

I started to look for him and called out but realized the time had already passed to be at the bus stop. Oh well. The girls could make it back to the house just fine and Jeff would have to miss his daily bus walk. Just as I was about to turn around to continue looking for him, I heard a small bang under the kitchen cabinet. I moved closer to the cabinet, opening it slowly. The last thing I wanted to see was a mouse. I could deal with a lot of things, but I hated mice. I opened the door to a wide-eyed Jeff, jelly jar in hand, smeared all over his face, hands and even on the top of his head. I was so mad I could see lightning flash in my eyes.

"Jeffrey Neil, do you understand that you are a mess? You are eating jelly and you are going to get sick not to mention we need this jelly for later. What were you thinking?!" I couldn't stop. I was yelling at Jeff as he stuck out his bottom lip and started to wail. He pointed his little finger behind me and looked past my shoulders. I turned to see Barbara Ann, who had walked in straight from school.

As soon as she saw Jeff, she panicked, thinking the jelly was blood running down his head and face, covering his little hands. Jeff wailed louder, Barbara screamed, "Mom! We have to get him to the HOSPITAL!" I laughed at all of it and both kids just wailed louder, probably thinking I was out of my mind.

I grabbed Barbara by the shoulders firmly and intently looking into her eyes, explained that it was only strawberry jelly that covered her little brother. The realization settled over her face as she relaxed and we both coaxed Jeff out of the cabinet straight into the bath. It was a moment I don't think any of us ever forgot.

GRANDMA SCARBOROUGH (ELVIRA)-YOU NEVER REALLY KNOW

"A friend loves at all times, and a brother is born
for a time of adversity." Proverbs 17:17 (NIV)

Things were not as easy as they used to be since the stroke. It was mainly frustrating. The things that I used to do that took both hands or anything intricate like sewing or lacing up shoes, rendered me helpless or at least trying with only one good side for about three times as long as it normally would have.

But there was always Nita Maxine. She would see a need and try to meet it, especially with me. She had talked to me a few times about her own mother. I remember one time sitting on the front porch, waiting for the kids to get home from school. Nita seemed sad, upset even, like she was angry. I had tried to feel her out for what was on her mind, but she wouldn't budge.

Finally, she looked at me and said, "I sometimes wish you were my mom. I mean you are because of Cliff but I miss her sometimes. I can't always remember her mannerisms and her voice; I don't want to lose the memories that I have."

She looked down at her hands and I put my hand over hers and told her what I felt deep in my heart, "Honey, God puts people in our lives because He knows we need 'em. You'll always need your momma but since she isn't here, I'm the next best thing." I gave her hands a squeeze and I winked at her. "You're stuck with me so I'm sorry about that."

She smiled and laughed a little. She moved on from that emotion as quickly as it started over her. She never sat in her feelings that long. That always worried me about her, too busy sometimes to feel. We women are like that sometimes.

I looked up from the chair I was sitting on in the front living room. I gave her a half smile and lifted my good arm. Nita had just walked in the door, sweeping in to help with lunch. She smiled at me, and I couldn't help but think that you never really know how much things can change. The good Lord knows what we need in all seasons, even if we really have no clue.

ANNALEE-REUNION TIME

---

*"Children's children are a crown to the aged, and parents
are the pride of their children." Proverbs 17:6 (NIV)*

I remember going to Grandview State Park as a kid for our annual Scarborough Family reunions. Honestly, I loved it. I didn't really know a lot of my extended family but there was something that piqued my curiosity knowing that I had family in places like Ohio, Texas, Virginia, and Florida.

Looking back, I don't think I took too much time to get to know my extended family and social media and email wasn't a thing so if I ever did want to communicate it was through snail mail or telephone. I don't think the younger kids ever had intentions of truly becoming best friends with our second or third cousins twice removed or whatever, but we surely enjoyed those times together.

I remember the rhododendron bushes that lined the trails at Grandview, the caves we climbed through to find "Hoofus Scoofus" and "Bloody Eyes" (thanks for that, dad) and great aunts and uncles that asked me lots of questions that I tried to answer carefully before running off to play on the playground beside the picnic shelter.

My mom would always make a cake for the reunion, mainly because we had requested the cake. Specifically, it was a sour cream pound cake. The name doesn't make this cake sound like much, but it was a marvel of dense cake, a layer of crunchy crust on the top and the best sweet taste you could imagine-no icing needed. Sometimes mom would put strawberries on it but it really didn't even need those. My mom would make this cake upon our request for the reunion almost every year. We loved this because everyone else opted for the gooey, iced desserts and sweets. Our cake would sit stoically, waiting for a customer. Usually there were only a few pieces taken by those who knew the enormity of taste this cake provided. We left the reunion, with a lovely cake in hand waiting to be devoured at home.

The reunion was interesting to me too because I caught a glimpse of who my dad and his siblings had been before I knew them. I would listen to stories about them growing up around cousins and mischief that they would get into. I listened to them sing songs and strum guitars- usually my dad and his cousin Steve. When you're little, you only see people how they are to you-mom, dad, uncle or aunt so and so, but the reunions made me realize these people were kids once too, making good choices and maybe some not great ones from time to time.

As a teen I would remember complaining about them, wanting to be somewhere else, but as soon as I got there, I loved it, I loved my family, the nostalgia, the stories I would hear from my great aunts and uncles, the overlook at Grandview and that sour cream pound cake we got to take home.

I miss these reunions. They stopped having them years ago. The older Scarborough's were either too old to make a trek to West Virginia or many had passed away. Others had different lives, taking them in different directions and places, with little time and space for a reunion again.

One thing that my dad and his siblings have done is to have dinner together every month or so. They take turns hosting the dinners and they just get together, catch up with each other and their spouses, and eat a good meal. I have never been to one of these dinners since I'm so far away now, but I love that they do this. The intentionality to meet and just be with each other is important.

There is a feeling we have around our family that is like nothing else. Family can frustrate and hurt us at times, tensing our shoulders and giving us aching heads. Mostly though, I think being around family is like an exhale, knowing that the people around you know you, they still love you and more than that, they want to be with you.

Nita Maxine-Good Neighbors

---

*"Love your neighbor, yet pull not down
your hedge." English Proverb*

I remember when Cliff's mom passed away. I was so sad and even more lonely. I had loved her, still loved her, as my very own mother. We spent many afternoons on the back porch just talking about life, watching the kids play. She had given me the best life advice, she had prayed for my kids and told them as much. I know she prayed for her own children even though they were grown now. I'll always think of her beautiful white hair that she would braid and pile on the top of her head. Her spirit was more beautiful than that.

I was hoping that the house wouldn't sit long without anyone in it. We had so many kids and family members on our street already. It felt safe and like home. I couldn't bear to think of a cranky old neighbor taking Ms. Scarborough's place.

It wasn't long after her passing and my fretting over who would move in beside us that Cliff told me his sister Marie, and her husband Ted were moving into his mom's house. I was instantly relieved.

As the weeks went by Marie and Ted finally moved in and settled. I was doing dishes one evening and I heard a knock on the door. I opened it to find Marie standing there with a cup of coffee. "Want to sit outside for a little, Maxine?" I smiled and we spent that evening catching up. I knew this would be the first of many more times sitting on the back porch with Marie. I was so thankful for good neighbors, good family and family that could be friends.

Joan, Barbara, Linda, David and Jeff-Gardens

"...for He satisfies the thirsty and fills the hungry
with good things." Psalm 107:9 *(NIV)*

We always had a garden. Even if the harvest wasn't always great, we planted and tended year to year. We would plant tomatoes, corn, potatoes, and green beans. We also had grapes, yellow and red cherries. We had honey from the bees that dad kept.

Every single family member had to help out with the garden. When it was time to harvest the garden, it was all hands on deck. We used much of what we canned from the garden to feed us throughout the year. Gathered in the small basement of the house on Hedrick Street, we would shuck corn, string beans and clean vegetables until we had completed the task. Grandma Scarborough would always come over and ask if mom could use some help and of course mom gladly took the help.

We had an old gas stove that we used to can the vegetables on. The work was hard and tedious but we looked forward to the harvest times. Everyone would gather tightly together, talking and laughing and working side by side. Those are some of the sweetest memories.

JEFF-GYPSY

"Do you know what love is? and he concludes,
"Sure I know. A boy and his dog." from
"A Boy and His Dog" by Harlan Ellison

I had always wanted a dog, I think maybe most boys do. I was eight when the fever hit me full throttle. It was like every kid in the neighborhood had a dog except for us. Mrs. Lilly let us play with her dog Blondie who was always roaming the neighborhood. She was a terrier type dog with unruly, curly hair that hung in her eyes. She would play around with me when I went over to Mrs. Lilly's house to do odd jobs, like rake leaves in the fall.

One day, God must have smiled down on me because Mrs. Lilly said that Blondie was going to have puppies and I could have one. My heart leapt out of my chest when she told me that and I ran back home hollering to mom and dad about Blondie and her pups. I didn't quite understand that I would have to convince my parents to let me have this puppy in the first place.

From that day forward, I tried to be on my best behavior to get this puppy. I also cried around a lot and made my parents feel like I might die if I didn't get a dog. Maybe it was the constant whining about the dog or maybe they figured they would see if I was up to the challenge of taking care of a dog, but finally it happened. My parents said yes to one of Blondie's puppies.

The day for Blondie to give birth could not have come any slower. It felt like years between my parents agreeing to a dog and the actual birth of my puppy. One day Mrs. Lilly called to me as I was walking down the road near her house. She told me that Blondie had had her puppies, but I needed to wait six more weeks before I could get my puppy. I had thought I would get one immediately but now, another six weeks?! I could hardly stand it.

I guess some things are worth the wait because as soon as I ended up getting my puppy which I named, "Gypsy", she never left my side. She ran through the woods with me when I played with other kids, she was always by my side as I roamed the neighborhood. All my friends knew "Jeff and Gypsy" because we were a package deal. She looked a lot like her mom with black and white hair. I learned about taking care of something besides myself with Gypsy and she lived seventeen years. Maybe she would have lived longer had "the incident" never happened but I think she may have used up an extra few years with this one…

Gypsy was running around like all puppies do, underfoot, too small, and always in the way. We were heading to Florida for vacation to see Aunt Nola. I had been playing baseball at the time and it seemed like I had a game up to the minute we left, and dad was working his last shift in the mines before we hit the road. It was chaotic to say the least, plus there was Gypsy.

The night before we left, amid the chaos, dad ran out to get a haircut. He sat behind the wheel of our Ford station wagon and began to pull out of the driveway. As he backed down the driveway, we all heard the high-pitched scream of a dog. Gypsy who was only about twelve weeks at the time, had decided to run behind the wheel of the car.

It was one of those moments in life you never forget. Besides the death of a family member or friend, a family pet can rip your heart out. I ran to see what had happened thinking I would have to say goodbye to the sweet puppy I had just really met. My heart shattered as dad told me to put her in a box and keep an eye on her and we would take her to the vet before we left if she got worse. She was breathing and seemed to be okay as she fell asleep in the little makeshift box bed. I remember crying and how hard it was to breathe. I guess I was feeling a true heart break for the first time.

We ate dinner that night, I probably didn't eat much, and after that I went to check on Gypsy. The box I had put her in was empty and she was running around the garage. I had to laugh and think about the fact that maybe cats aren't the only ones with nine lives!

Gypsy ended up living around seventeen or eighteen years and when I left home, mom and dad took over all the Gypsy responsibilities. David helped out too. She was a good dog and I'd like to think Gypsy and the other pets that I have loved in this life will be roaming around heaven with me one day.

JEFF-SLEIGH RIDES AND
HITCHING RIDES

"For He orders His angels to protect you wherever you go. They will hold you with their hands to keep you from striking your foot on a stone." Psalm 91:11-12 (NLT)

It's funny how a thing can change. Something that seemed so large and looming as a kid, pales in comparison as an adult. I drove by Kessinger's Hill a few years back and it is just like any other ordinary hill, not grand by any means.

I loved that place as a kid. As soon as the first snowfall hit, we would go to Kessy's Hill (that's what we called it) and ride sleds all day. A fire would be made so we could stand by and keep warm when we weren't riding down the hill. All the kids would bundle up and meet at the top of the hill. We used regular sleds and car hoods turned over so they would be able to fly down the hill. To go to Kessinger's Hill was like a little taste of freedom for us kids. We usually spent the most time there during Christmas breaks.

On snowy days we would also hitch rides to get to the L&B Supermarket just down the road. We could have always walked down the road but even better was hitching a ride. Now, I'm not talking about thumbing a ride and getting into a car, but actually getting on the back bumper of a car as it slowed down and letting it pull us on the back. Sometimes we would just hang on and slide on our feet through the snow. Going down Ashworth's hill on the back of a car was the best because you could get a pretty long ride and let go right before the car or truck would get to the L&B.

We never got hurt so I'm pretty sure we had plenty of guardian angels hanging out on our street too. Thank goodness mom and dad didn't know we did that because I'm not so sure a guardian angel would have done much good then.

NITA MAXINE-DIFFERENT ISN'T BAD

"Thank you for making me so wonderfully complex! Your workmanship is marvelous-how well I know it." Psalm 139:14 (NLT)

Elbert Lee Pack was my cousin. He lived close to the family as we grew up on Hedrick Street. He was beside the Farrish's across from the little church on the main road. Elbert was an interesting person in the fact that he was both deaf and mute. I remember the kids being a little scared of Elbert Lee.

He was big and strange and the sounds he made were not sounds that you would expect from a grown man. I admired Elbert though. He had worked hard all of his life and probably always went the extra mile. He had been made fun of and left out many times, but he still went about his life, that's all he could do I guess.

Elbert Lee was eventually married and he and his wife never had kids so he doted on our kids. Elbert Lee helped anyone he could and had a kind heart. He helped Cliff with the new addition and was a decent carpenter. He was also extremely strong.

Elbert Lee would always be a bit of a Pack Town legend as the story goes that one time when he was working on his 1957 Chevy station wagon, the car fell off the jacks somehow pinning Elbert Lee underneath it. Instead of panicking, he was able to push the car up enough to roll out from under it with only a few broken ribs. The people in the neighborhood always talked about Elbert's strength when they saw him or if someone mentioned him.

To most, Elbert was a man you kept at a distance. Keeping things at a distance seems safe especially when that person is misunderstood. Sometimes I would sit with him during services at the Regular Baptist Church on Johnstown Road. Most people would avoid eye contact because talking to someone who is deaf and mute seemed nearly impossible during those times. If Elbert was walking home from church, I would give him a ride. Elbert knew a lot of things and was an intelligent man. It's unfortunate that so many people never knew that simply because he was different.

A FEW WORDS TO END

I would say that there are so many more stories that could be told. I wish I could have told more. Maybe some that are worth telling and some worth tucking. Worth tucking away, to savor and hold close, or worth tucking because putting them on paper won't really change anything. That's the thing, memories can't be changed but how we all remember something can be wildly different.

I saw the differences in memory when I began to ask my family for stories about grandma and grandpa and growing up. Our perspectives change as we grow, and I think my grandparents had changed a lot from Linda all the way to David. Time can grow you up, mellow you out and shift your priorities. I think that's what happened to my grandparents. I think it's what really happens to all of us. I think that's the beauty of life, that God gives second chances and allows us to change, He loves us despite ourselves. He is the One Who knows our deepest secrets and loves us most.

Grandma wasn't perfect and would never want anyone to think that was my perception of her or the reason for writing these little stories of remembrance. These stories aren't written because they are perfect, or the people in them are perfect. They are written because they are about the imperfect people who came before me, who are still here, who have taught me and are continuing to teach me about the beauty that comes from everyday, normal, imperfect lives. They are stones of remembrance for me and hopefully to anyone who spends the few minutes it takes to read this little book.

Reflecting on my family's lives has made me so appreciative of where I come from. The hard work, determination, perseverance, and grit my family members have shown in many ways as I have observed them, reminds me that I can do whatever I want to do, even in my now, middle age.

My family has lived through wars, the Civil Rights Movement, recessions, terrorist attacks, a pandemic, political turmoil-not to mention what was happening in their own personal lives. Their stories are so important and worth capturing.

In the last talks I had with Grandma, before she really couldn't talk anymore, she was so very proud of every one of her children, grandchildren, and great grandchildren. She would have said that one of the biggest parts of her, one of her life's largest accomplishments, was them, was us.

So here's to all the stories we have stored up in our hearts, the ones on the pages, the ones we will write and the ones that will be written about us.

"Seventy years are given to us! Some may even reach eighty. But even the best of these years are filled with pain and trouble: soon they disappear and we are gone." Psalm 90:10 (NLT)

PICTURES OF THE PAST

"Time can play all sorts of tricks on you. In the
blink of an eye, babies appear in carriages, coffins
disappear into the ground, wars are won and lost,
and children transform, like butterflies, into adults."-
Brian Selznick, The Invention of Hugo Cabret

*Nita Maxine Scarborough (Pittman) and Clifford Dura
Scarborough in the early years right after they were married*

Grandpa (Clifford Dura Scarborough) in his army uniform

(Grandpa) Clifford and his brothers, from left- Woody, Cliff, Glover and George

1965- Barbara, Linda, Jeff (crutches), Joan and David (front)

Great Grandma Pittman, Nita's mom-died of kidney failure at age 41

WITHHOLDING TAX STATEMENT **1963** Copy C—For Employee's Records
Federal Taxes Withheld From Wages

SOCIAL SECURITY INFORMATION		INCOME TAX INFORMATION		WEST VIRGINIA	
F. I. C. A. employee tax withheld, if any	Total F. I. C. A. Wages paid in 1963	Federal Income Tax Withheld, if any	Total Wages (before payroll deductions or "sick pay" exclusion) paid in 1963	Personal Income Tax Withheld, if any	
21.62	595.20	none	595.20		
				W. Va. Wages Paid if different from Federal Wages	

Type or print
EMPLOYEE'S
Social
security
account
number,
name, and
address

236 32 3094

. Mits Maxine Scarborough
. Beckley, W. Va.

Type or print EMPLOYER'S identification number, name, and address below

55-0462480

NOTICE: If your wages were subject to Social Security taxes, but are not shown, your Social Security wages are the same as wages shown under "INCOME TAX INFORMATION", but not more than $4,800. Keep this copy as part of your tax records.

Lorena Stanley, dba,
Stanley's Dairy Bar
Beckley, W. Va.

FORM W-2—U. S. Treasury Department, Internal Revenue Service

A 1963 tax withholding statement from Lorena Stanley's Dairy Bar when Grandma worked there

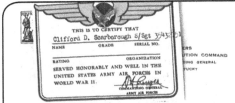

THIS IS TO CERTIFY THAT

Clifford D. Scarborough S/Sgt 3-432151

NAME   GRADE   SERIAL NO.

RATING   ORGANIZATION

SERVED HONORABLY AND WELL IN THE
UNITED STATES ARMY AIR FORCES IN
WORLD WAR II.

COMMANDING GENERAL
ARMY AIR FORCES

...ERS
...UTION COMMAND
...DING GENERAL
...TUCKY

To Former Members of the AAF Team:

    General Arnold has directed that I write to inform you that even
though you no longer wear the Air Forces uniform, we of the Air Forces
consider you one of us.

    The tremendous accomplishment of the Air Forces was only made
possible by contributions such as you made.

    We wish that we could make all Air Force facilities available
to you, however, we are prohibited by regulations from doing so.
There are limitations to the assistance we can be to you, but we
wish you to know that there is a trained Air Force officer at each
base to assist our present and former personnel in the handling of
their personal affairs.

    We would be glad to have you contact the Personal Affairs officer
at the nearest Air Force base if you have a problem which you feel he
can help you solve.

                     Sincerely,

                     H. R. HARMON
                     Major General, U.S.A.
                     Commanding

*A letter to the former members of the AAF who
fought in WWII (to my grandpa Clifford)*

1970-Jeff, Linda, Barbara, Joan and David
(taken at Grandview, WV)

Glover, Woody, Cliff (Grandpa Scarborough), Marie, Elsie, Mossie and Grandma Scarborough (Elvira-my great grandma, Cliff's mom)

My Great Grandma Scarborough, Cliff's mom (Elvira)

My grandpa (far left) and some of his army air force buddies cutting loose for a bit. Maybe these were some of the guys that covered for him when he was off base for the wedding.

Grandpa (Clifford) and a war buddy-grandpa had bet his buddy that he couldn't fit into the tail gunner seat of a B-17 where my grandpa usually sat. My grandpa lost the bet.

Jeff, his mom (Nita Maxine), Linda, in front: Joan and Barabara (Circa 1988-I think by the clothes and hair)

*Jeff, Nita Maxine and her sister Nola at Linda's house
for a July 4th celebration in West Virginia (2002)*

George and Harriet Elvira Scarborough (my grandpa's parents)

One of the last formal pictures of my grandma
(She was 86 years young in this one.)

*An early picture of my grandpa as a baby and
some of his siblings-Elsie, George, Glover*

*A picture of me (the baby in grandpa's arms), and all
my cousins with our grandparents at the Scarborough
reunion at Grandview State Park, WV (1980)*

*Andrew is in grandma's arms, Laura and Angie
are in front being cute little girls-Angie is sucking
her thumb and has her arm around Laura*

*Me at the Scarborough reunion on a swing-you can
see dad in the background (circa 1984)*

Me, Brian and grandma at our wedding at
Foxwood Inn (June 28, 2003)

*My mom and grandpa sitting together and laughing at one of
the family's birthday get togethers. My grandpa always loved
my mom and she had a special place in her heart for him.*

Grandma laughing and opening a card- she was probably pretty happy about the cupcake too. This was after she had gotten sick and my dad and his siblings, along with a home health nurse, were taking care of her. This was the year she passed away and I think this was around her birthday in August 2021. She always loved gifts and cake.

Grandpa and Great Uncle Ted Floyd (Marie's husband) riding horses. I love this picture. It makes me think of cowboys.

*Barbara and Grandma on one of her
traveling adventures (circa 1997)*

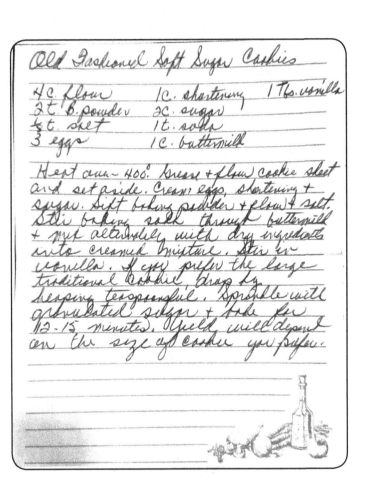

Old Fashioned Soft Sugar Cookies

4 c. flour	1 c. shortening	1 Tbs. vanilla
2 t. b. powder	2 c. sugar	
½ t. salt	1 t. soda	
3 eggs	1 c. buttermilk	

Heat oven ~ 400°. Grease + flour cookie sheet and set aside. Cream eggs, shortening + sugar. Sift baking powder + flour + salt. Stir baking soda through buttermilk + mix alternately with dry ingredients into creamed mixture. Stir in vanilla. If you prefer the large traditional cookie, drop by heaping teaspoonful. Sprinkle with granulated sugar + bake for 12-15 minutes. Yield will depend on the size of cookie you prefer.

Grandma's (Nita Maxine's) Sugar cookie recipe-Even though we would all love her ever elusive roll recipe, this will have to do!

One Last Story-Grandpa Scarborough (Clifford)

"To laugh often and much; to win the respect of intelligent people and the affection of children; to earn the appreciation of honest critics and endure the betrayal of false friends; to appreciate the beauty; to find the best in others; to leave the world a bit better, whether by a healthy child, a garden patch or a redeemed social condition; to know even one life has breathed easier because you have lived. This is to have succeeded!"-Emerson

I would like to think that we had a good life. I would like to think I gave them all that and they in turn gave themselves that. I would like to think that despite the many words I never said, they knew I loved them, I cherished being with them. It was hard to express feelings sometimes, but I know I felt love for them all. They were all so unique and different in their own ways. They still are. I watched them grow up, have their own lives and they all made me proud. Yes, there were times they also frustrated me or made me sad, but I loved them above it all.

Times have changed so much. I have seen horses become cars and people become wilder and freer and less disciplined than I ever thought humans could be. I have seen the invention of computers and mobile phones. I have seen this little street grow up and all of Beckley with it. I have lived through a war that I should have died in and I still have memories of that war I would never wish on anyone. There have been more recent wars I have read about in the newspapers or heard about on the nightly news. Sometimes I feel this country is falling apart at the seams and sometimes I am prouder than ever to live here. I have seen my parents come and go, siblings as well. I have worked in the West Virginia coal mines and I have been a disabled man, golfing and selling real estate. I have lived a hundred lives and yet I am here, sitting in this backyard porch, the sun shining, listening to chatter of my family.

Now as I sit here and watch the grandkids play, running around the backyard, after eating sugary cake and ice cream and watching Nita open her gifts, I can't help but wonder what these kids will turn out to be like, and even their kids. Life comes at us fast and hard and full circle. I think they'll be okay. I pray they will anyways. I do that a lot more these days, pray. I never let anyone know about that, but I do, I've always worked out my own faith quietly.

I tilt my head back, adjusting my straw hat, and squint into the sun as one of my grandkids runs up to me and asks me a question about the tree in our back yard. I pat his back and tell him he can run around the big willow tree and hide under it too, if he can climb it, that would be even better, I tell him, just be careful.

This is life and living, so full of goodness and sometimes sadness, full of the people I love, often missing those that aren't here. I am thankful for it all. I smile and turn back to my wife and my kids.

About the Author

Annalee was born in Southern West Virginia. A child of the eighties, she loved Lisa Frank notebooks and smelly stickers. She has lived in four different states and although she tried for years to get rid of her West Virginia accent, she has realized that where you are from is one of the most important things about you. Annalee enjoys writing, reading multiple books at one time, being a mom to two beautiful children and helping her beloved husband find things around the house. She lives in Colorado where she spends as much time as possible on mountains, walking around her neighborhood or pretending she is best friends with her Peloton instructors. In her spare time she teaches English to children and adults. She is active in her local church where she teaches women about Jesus as often as possible. She is inspired to tell stories and help other people tell their own.

Printed in the United States
by Baker & Taylor Publisher Services